THE Power of an Hour

THE Power
of an
Hour

BUSINESS AND LIFE MASTERY IN ONE HOUR A WEEK

DAVE LAKHANI

WILEY

John Wiley & Sons, Inc.

Published by John Wiley & Sons, Inc., Hoboken, New Jersey.
Published simultaneously in Canada.

For general information on our other products and services or for technical support, please contact
our Customer Care Department within the United States at (800) 762-2974, outside the United
States at (317) 572-3993 or fax (317) 572-4002.

Wiley also publishes its books in a variety of electronic formats. Some content that appears in print
may not be available in electronic books. For more information about Wiley products, visit our
web site at www.wiley.com.

Library of Congress Cataloging-in-Publication Data:

Lakhani, Dave, 1965–
    The power of an hour: business and life mastery in one hour a week / Dave
Lakhani.
        p.   cm.
    Includes index.
    ISBN-13: 978-0-471-78093-9 (cloth)
    ISBN-10: 0-471-78093-6 (cloth)
    1. Executive ability.   2. Success in business.   3. Organizational change.
I. Title.
HD38.2.L345 2006
658.4'09—dc22

                                                        2005033008

Printed in the United States of America.

10   9   8   7   6   5   4   3   2

This book is dedicated with love to Stephanie and Austria, who make my life the wonder and joy it is today.

It is also dedicated to my family: Suleman Lakhani, Pavreen Lakhani, Jehan Lakhani, and Imran Lakhani.

Finally, to my very good friends, MSG Dennis Stockwell, Al Murray, and Mark Ernst.

Contents

Foreword

When you carefully study the most successful businesses in the world or the most successful people, as I have, you'll see that they have one thing in common . . . a drive to incrementally improve every day, every month, every year. And when you look at people who would be successful or who have businesses that could be successful but aren't, you see them struggle because they are unclear or unsure about what to focus on. They know that they should be taking some action, but they don't know where to start. They continue to do the same things every day. They are paralyzed, and inaction kills.

This book solves that problem in a very actionable way.

Focus, consistency, and action.

Those are the keys to growing your business or yourself.

But let me ask you one powerful question, and I want you to answer it honestly. Do you know exactly what you could focus on for one hour that would dramatically change your life or your business?

The Power of an Hour reveals the most important things that you must do to develop focus, it compels you to action, and it gives you the master plan for consistent movement forward in your business or your life.

Anyone who reads this book and applies the ideas inside will hold the master keys to creating incremental improvements in business and personal success every day in every crucial area of life and business. *The Power of an Hour* does an amazing job of breaking down critical personal and business issues (which are nearly always tied closely together) into very clear focus points that allow you to choose what is most important for you to focus on and to have the tools you need to create tremendous momentum.

As you read *The Power of an Hour* and begin focusing for an hour at a time, you'll experience amazing results. As you continue to practice, you'll do something else: You'll condition your mind and you'll learn how to focus, create momentum, and improve fast.

Take this book with you right now and read it.

Then, spend one hour in Fearsome Focus (which you'll learn more about in the book) and focus on the most important chapter in the book for you. Stay focused on momentum and achievement. Incremental improvement will be yours, and that very improvement will allow you to dominate your market and yourself.

So, I want to ask you again: Do you know exactly what you could focus on for one hour that would dramatically change your life or your business?

I strongly suggest that you start by reading this book.

Then, pick the most important hour of focus from the book and get started.

You'll be glad you did, and your business will be glad you did.

And you'll finally understand what it means to work *on* your business or your life, not just *in* it.

Take action now.

> —T. Harv Eker
> Author of the *New York Times* bestseller
> *Secrets of the Millionaire Mind*

Preface

This book is like no other business book or personal development book you've ever read and I'm proud of that. The last thing you need is another formulaic book you could have written yourself. This book is holistic; it addresses both personal and business issues because there is no separation between the two. If one side suffers, by necessity so does the other.

This book is different because it's designed to work with a busy executive's or business owner's schedule. Each chapter is meant to stand alone and offers a complete how-to process from start to finish. Use it an hour at a time or a project at a time but, most important, use it.

In my work with corporate executives, whether of Fortune 500 companies or small businesses, I've found that they all have one thing in common—they want to create change. Often the change they have in mind is inside their own organization. What they repeatedly discover is that in order to create change in their organization or team, they must first create it in themselves.

In both cases, organizational and personal, there are common areas that impact all business owners. If your business isn't growing and performing the way you want, you suffer. If you are suffering, your business can't grow and perform optimally.

I've developed a plan for change that I've taught and used for more than 10 years. In developing the program, I knew the only way it would work was if it didn't take a lot of time and if the results were quickly obvious. The program works if you simply take the steps and apply them one at a time, an hour at a time.

The Power of an Hour is designed to be broken down into the most manageable blocks of time, a single hour. While this isn't a time management book, it covers time management issues so you can make the most of your Power Hours.

The Power of an Hour provides the structure necessary to create powerful change in one single hour. It stimulates thinking about what is needed in specific areas of your business or career. I've covered the areas of marketing, sales, management, and others that most impact our lives. I've also explored the areas of personal life that cause the most stress to work, health, and relationships. And, while I don't profess to be an expert on relationships or health, I am an expert on demonstrating the best questions to ask in order to create a powerful solution for those areas of your life. In addition, I've introduced industry experts who share their particular views on what you can do in an hour to improve your personal and professional lives. They have included some of the most effective questions to ask and answer for yourself for creating positive change. I've even got an expert who'll improve your golf game (he was one of Phil Mickelson's college golf coaches; he knows a thing or two about creating winners).

This book is a guidebook. Open the book to the issue you want to focus on and you'll find detailed information about the key areas you should explore. The first part of the book teaches the Power of an Hour process that leads you to the state I refer to as Fearsome Focus.

Fearsome Focus came about as a result of my previous experience as a professional kickboxer and as a former law enforcement officer who worked in undercover narcotics and on SWAT (special weapons and tactics) teams. I learned that in violent encounters you have to be intensely focused for short periods of time in order not just to succeed, but to survive. I later discovered that when I applied the same level of focus to my work or my personal life, I was able to accomplish what many others around me could not. I began sharing the concept of Fearsome Focus with other business owners and they found that, by truly focusing, they accomplished things that had been hanging over them for months or even years. They were able to get results they hadn't in the past because they finally understood the effects of being single-minded in their effort to create and succeed.

Throughout the chapters in this book, I hope both to change your thinking about what is possible in a single hour and also to persuade you to truly evaluate what *you* can accomplish in that hour.

I hope to inspire you to make the next hour your most powerful and meaningful, whether you use it to change yourself or your business. Everyone gets the same number of minutes in an hour. What you do with them and how you invest them will ultimately determine what you'll get out of all the hours in your life.

Acknowledgments

There are many people who helped with this book and who have supported me though the process, none more important than Matt Holt at Wiley. Matt kept me on track and focused while I promoted another book that was released while I was writing this one. Matt is simply the best editor a writer could hope for.

I am grateful to Joe Vitale for all he has done to make my books come to life and be successful once they are in print. Everyone should have a Joe Vitale in his life.

I also acknowledge the contributions of Dr. David Sim, Wendy Luiso, Tom and Lisa Brill, Joe Santana, Glenn Dietzel, Randy Gilbert, Armand Mornin, Alex Mandossian, Len Foley, and Jill Lublin.

This book was more challenging to write than my first one, since I took on speaking engagements and promotional efforts to support the first book, plus other tasks associated with having a new book and one in the works. At times I was absent, irritable, abnormally funny, and often simply unavailable. I deeply appreciate my wife, Stephanie, for keeping things going and my daughter, Austria, for always being ready with a kiss for dad.

Thanks to Elizabeth Belts for a great job editing the first drafts.

And of course I thank all of my family, including my Grandmother, Edith Ramsey Johnson, and my brothers, Bill Willard, Jr. and Micah Willard. You have made my life an exceptional adventure.

Finally, I send appreciation to all my clients past, present, and future. It is the experiences I have with you that make these books possible.

About the Author

Dave Lakhani is the world's first Business Acceleration Strategist and President of Bold Approach, Inc., a Business Acceleration Strategy firm that helps companies worldwide to immediately increase their revenue through effective sales, marketing, and public relations.

Considered one of the world's top experts on the application of persuasion, Dave gives lectures that are in high demand by corporations and trade organizations of all sizes. His advice is regularly seen in *Selling Power* magazine, *Sales and Marketing Management*, the *Wall Street Journal*, *Investor's Business Daily*, *Inc.*, *Entrepreneur*, the *Today* show, and many other media outlets. Dave is also the host of Making Marketing Work, a radio talk show focused on marketing strategy for growing businesses. Dave has written *Persuasion: The Art of Getting What You Want* (Wiley, 2005); *A Fighting Chance* (Prince Publishing, 1991); a section of the anthology *Ready, Aim, Hire* (Persysco, 1992); and the audio book, *Making Marketing Work* (BA Books, 2004).

Dave has owned more than 10 successful businesses in the last 20 years and considers himself a serial entrepreneur and committed business builder. An avid student and lifelong learner, Dave has studied every major sales, marketing, or influence professional in the past 20 years. He's a Master Practitioner of Neuro-Linguistic Programming (NLP) who has studied with NLP's founder, Richard Bandler, and he is also a graduate and former adjunct faculty member of the Wizard of Ads Academy.

Dave lives in Boise, Idaho, with his wife, Stephanie, and his daughter, Austria. When not on the road with clients or making speeches, Dave enjoys scuba diving, skiing, martial arts, reading, and great wine.

Visit Dave online at www.powerofanhour.com.

The Power of an Hour

Change

Whether you own a business or just want to be the best person you can, you must subject yourself to change. Every day in my business I talk to business owners and corporate leaders who are working diligently to find time to create the change needed in their own businesses. Many also feel they'd be more effective if they were able to create personal change as well. But ultimately, what holds everyone back is time.

While time may seem like the thing you need the most of, it turns out that isn't true. What you need is focus—a very specific kind of focus. I'm going to help you find that focus in your personal life and in your business as you read the coming chapters. You'll get practical step-by-step advice, and you'll get expert instruction from highly qualified specialists, who will show you exactly what to do and when to do it. Most important, they'll show you how to structure your activity so you are always able to achieve exactly the results you want.

How the Power of an Hour Works

Saying in the previous paragraph that time isn't the real issue will leave many of you scratching your head, when you consider the name of the book, so let me elaborate.

We all get the same number of minutes and hours in a day to work, create, live, and prosper. It's how we use those hours that makes the real difference in terms of the quality of our lives and the value of our businesses.

In order to create the kind of change that achieves truly meaningful goals, the focus must be on what I call the Critical Power Hour™. I focus on a single hour because virtually anyone can extract himself from the rigors of daily life and invest one hour a day to create change. An hour is also the easiest quantity of time for us to schedule. Finally, I chose an hour because, after 15 years of helping people realize their business and personal goals, I've come to realize it only takes an hour to initiate change. Any more than an hour of real focus without a break results in a rapid breakdown in productivity. After an hour of intense focus, the mind begins to wander, excuses come to the surface, and restarting is harder than ever because of the amount of effort you've expended beyond an hour. I've also chosen an hour because it works. In virtually every business I've worked with, when I get people to use this process they achieve exponential results. Also, by limiting your focus to an hour, you will be able to immediately see and feel the gratification that comes from completion once that hour is past.

I'm not saying there won't be times when it is necessary to focus for longer than an hour; however, those times should be limited. True focus is a marathon effort packed into a sprint. There is tremendous accomplishment at the end; there is also tremendous insight that occurs. I will cover more about that later in the book.

The Power of an Hour works because it limits the amount of time used and is focused in a specific way. Here are the steps of the Power of an Hour program that should be applied each time a new area of desired change is identified.

Seven Steps to Activating the Power of an Hour

1. Clearly identify what you need to change.
2. Apply critical thinking to identify the structure of the change.
3. Apply creative thinking to identify other solutions.
4. Identify next steps.
5. Schedule your change and take the first action.
6. Evaluate your activity and measure your success.
7. Reward your successful completion.

Let's take a closer look at each step in order to better understand it and how it applies. You must understand the steps because they will be the basis of your Power of an Hour system for success.

Clearly Identify What You Need to Change

Solving the wrong problem is one of the most significant reasons that real change does not occur. In order to create fast and lasting change, you must first take time to clearly identify the problems you want solved. Here are a few questions that need to be answered before a project is started.

- What is the specific factor initiating this change? In other words, what one thing contributed to this decision?
- Is that one thing important enough to focus your efforts and finances to achieve this change?

- Will this change lead to other changes that must occur as a result? If so, what areas?
- What would happen if the change does not solve your problem?
- What specifically needs to be changed?
- Who needs to be involved in order to create this change?
- What is the outcome that must be achieved as a result of this change?
- What does this mean to the organization financially, socially, environmentally, and organizationally?
- What does this mean to you personally? What specifically will you get from making this change?
- What will happen if this change does not occur?
- What is the best possible outcome of this change?
- Who, by name, will be impacted by the change?
- How will you define success?
- How will you reward successful completion of the change?

After working with hundreds of companies, I've found that by simply going through this checklist and challenging the answers, change is created more quickly. This happens because as you go through the list and discuss specifics, often the problem may not be real; it may be smaller than it appeared, or perhaps it was not necessary to solve it. If we decide that the problem really needs to be solved, that gives us valuable information about how to create the change.

This process does another thing too. It provides a complete understanding of who needs to be involved and held accountable. Finally, it informs you when you've been successful and reminds you to stop. Often, change doesn't work because those creating it don't know when to stop. The result is that the person or the organization that is changing can't see an end to the process and feels stuck in a state of flux. Successful change happens because there is a definite and defined end.

Apply Critical Thinking to Identify the Structure of Change

Critical thinking is such an important process that I'm dedicating an entire chapter to the topic (Chapter 3). Critical thinking needs to be applied early on in the process in order to break the change down to its smallest and most actionable items. Critical thinking also allows us to determine the best courses of action. Too often we start out with a new plan or idea that we are wildly enthusiastic about but fail to be realistic about requirements or outcomes. The result is that the idea dies on the vine. We've all experienced these failures in our personal lives when we resolve to diet, exercise, or stop smoking, for example. In business, when critical thinking is missing, we may start new revenue initiatives that don't take shape, or we create products that are never launched appropriately or never become as fully profitable as they could be. It's not that the idea isn't good; we simply failed to think it through appropriately in the Critical Power Hour.

Apply Creative Thinking to Identify Other Solutions

A problem I see, whether I am coaching individuals or consulting with business clients, is the idea of absolutes. Many times absolutes are the result of strongly held beliefs or a failure to consider other perspectives. Absolutes nearly always result in a less positive outcome than is possible.

Creative thinking is another skill that is so important I'll cover it in a separate chapter (Chapter 4). Challenging assumptions, beliefs, and absolutes for the purpose of seeing what else exists or is possible allows you to get the most out of your Critical Power Hour.

It is important you explore all of the alternatives that exist when you set out to create powerful change in a short period of time. Often you'll discover there are quicker, better, and more efficient solutions to the challenges you face. Many of us forget to look for creative solutions and only look to linear solutions that seem obvious.

Identify Next Steps

Now that you've identified what needs changing, why, and what the outcome could be, it's time to identify what to do next. It can be difficult for people to define what should be changed and what it can mean, because they focus on the result and abandon the process, hoping that someone else will pick up the pieces and make it happen. Unfortunately, it isn't quite that simple. You must identify the steps to be taken and document them. Be as specific as possible when documenting your next steps and assign specific completion times. Part of creating Fearsome Focus™ is knowing what to focus on and for how long. Undocumented next steps don't happen—it's that simple. Part of being able to create Fearsome Focus is the ability to redirect your focus back to the plan whenever necessary; if you don't have a plan you won't know where to refocus your efforts.

Schedule Your Change and Take the First Steps to Action

The most powerful action you can take in initiating change is to schedule and act. The reason you can create massive change in an hour is because of your ability to focus for an hour. But not all problems can be solved in a single hour; in fact, many of the initiatives you undertake in this process will take many hours. The key is to apply Fearsome Focus for an hour at a time.

Take your list of next steps and break them down into time commitments. If you need to schedule a session that will last more than an hour, here is what you can do:

- Schedule the block of time. You must be totally committed to this time; you have to treat it as one of the most important appointments you've ever made . . . because it is.
- Break the block into two segments of 45 and 15 minutes. Forty-five minutes are spent in Fearsome Focus and 15 minutes are spent at the end of the hour doing necessary nonfocus activities like returning e-mail, doing web research, taking a restroom break, or returning phone calls. At the end of 15 minutes, whatever is not complete gets moved forward to the next 15-minute segment (after the next Fearsome Focus).

You must be ruthless in following the 45/15 rule. There can be no interruptions in your Fearsome Focus time. Turn off your phone, close your e-mail, and turn off your cell phone. There is nothing so important that it can't wait 45 minutes. In the event some major issue arises, someone can come and physically interrupt you. Don't let intrusive and prevalent distractions destroy your focus.

The other reason that the time is broken down into 45 and 15-minute segments is that maintaining Fearsome Focus requires regular breaks so you can refresh your will and willingness to focus. It gives your mind a much-needed opportunity to relax, rejuvenate, and process all of the information you've just taken in. Often in these 15-minute intervals you'll have amazing breakthroughs.

I'm often asked if I use this process and the answer is unequivocally yes. I even used it for writing this book. I'm often asked what happens when I get writer's block, and my answer surprises many. I don't. I schedule my writing time and I apply Fearsome Focus. Whether I feel like writing or not, I start at my scheduled time. I have yet to find a time that I wasn't able to write effectively. Why? Simple—I've trained my brain and created a conditioned response that when I schedule time to write and all external distractions are removed, as long as I have set all my goals and created a plan of attack, I'm instantly able to write.

Initiating action ensures your success, so before you finish your Fearsome Focus session, whether it is a one-hour or a multiple-hour activity, complete one action right then.

If you plan to focus on your health and one of your identified steps is to contact a personal trainer, then pick up the phone and make the call. If you need to pull together a team for the change you want to create, then put the e-mail together identifying the team and send them the meeting notice. By taking one immediate action, you commit yourself physically (by the actual action), mentally (by starting a process), and emotionally (by acknowledging the feelings that getting started brings).

The only exception to the 45/15 rule is the initial Critical Power Hour. During the Critical Power Hour, you must remain focused for the entire hour. You may at the end of the hour use the 45/15 rule to initiate your first action.

Evaluate Your Activity and Measure Your Success

As you go through the process of creating change, you must regularly evaluate your activity. When evaluating, you need to compare it to the plan and to the timeline that you've set for yourself. By rigidly following this structure, you'll be insured of remaining on track and know that the focus being applied is contributing to the accomplishment of the goals set out for yourself or your team.

During your Critical Power Hour, it's necessary to measure activity and success. So the first evaluation is: Is everyone here that should be? If other people need to be involved in the Critical Power Hour and they are not there, then you need to immediately reschedule it so that everyone is present. There is no value in going over old ground with people who were not initially involved in the process and who aren't emotionally committed to what you've already created.

After you've scheduled time and are taking action, regularly evaluate the focus during the 45-minute segments to insure you're on task. By constantly checking progress against your documented next steps, you have regular feedback to guide you.

Measuring your success is a critical element to ensuring change. We often underestimate or overestimate the time the change will take or what assets and resources are required for success. For change to happen quickly, you must know what needs to change in your personal process and in the structure of your plan as early as possible. Measurement also reinforces a commitment to the project and provides great satisfaction when a job is being done properly and efficiently. Measurement allows you to predict the results of hard work before the final product is realized. Measurement is the key to long-term success in creating fast and permanent change.

Reward Your Successful Completion

It is said that a job well done is a reward in itself, but I believe that is only partially true. You may find inward satisfaction by what you've accomplished, but in any change there are others who participated in your success and they deserve recognition as well.

Celebrating and rewarding your success teaches you and your team that at the end of every worthy task there is cause for celebration! Conditioning your mind and behavior results in predictable success. Rewarding success brings teams together. Great bonding and ownership occur when you celebrate a success together. And, in the case of business, when others see a team celebrating their successes, they are much more likely to want to contribute to a winning team in the future.

Often I use a program called Mind Manager, from www.mindjet.com, to structure my thoughts. Mind Manager allows me to create a mind map that is a visual representation of what I plan to create and who needs to be involved. I can then print it out and carry it with me or publish it as a web page for everyone else to see. Mind Manager also gives me the opportunity to systemize my thinking process so that the moment I begin focusing for my Critical Power Hour I can start collecting my thoughts and see how they are all connected.

Your ability to create change is directly related to your ability to use the Power of an Hour process regularly. When you start structuring your hours according to this plan, you'll produce the blueprint for any change you want to accomplish.

How to Focus—
The Power
in the Hour

Focus, flow, and being in the zone are all the same experience. They define the ability to concentrate fully on a task with singlemindedness until it is complete. The ability to focus at will and consistently is a skill that many people will never take the time to develop. To maximize effort in an hour a week, I'm going to share my Fearsome Focus formula with you.

Fearsome Focus is the ability to constructively shut out all unwanted or undesirable outside stimuli and methodically move through a task. It is willingness to practice the skill over and over again until you develop brutal efficiency that insures your success. Fearsome Focus allows you to achieve any and every meaningful thing in your life; it is a skill that will set you apart from your peers and insure your success.

I first discovered and began developing the idea of Fearsome Focus when I was learning martial arts. The martial arts are composed of many different principles, many different physical maneuvers, and many predetermined responses to an opponent's action. But the most successful martial artists are not the ones who know the most techniques; they are the ones who have perfected a reasonable number of techniques and have practiced them over and over. The techniques are not just memorized, they are internalized. They are hard-coded into muscle memory so that the practitioner knows simply by the feel of the technique whether it was done correctly or not.

I found that the fastest way to internalize the techniques was through focused practice. Every day I would invest at least one hour in practicing the techniques I was learning. I'd practice them in the mirror, on the bag, or on my invisible sparring partner, George, and I'd practice them with a live opponent. I would discipline myself to do the same technique literally hundreds of times until it was wired into my body, so that no matter what the circumstance I could respond.

I also learned not to let other people's plans or attacks disrupt my plan. When I fought I focused on fighting my plan. I focused on responding to my opponent's attack in a way that ensured a predetermined outcome; success was mine because of my ability to focus. Pain could not disrupt my focus, a change of strategy on the part of the other person could not change my focus, and fear could not change my focus. Only I could change my focus, and I had trained myself to change my focus only when the encounter was over.

When you are in a state of Fearsome Focus, you can feel it wash over you. It is real—it fills your muscles, your mind, your thoughts. It doesn't direct you; it drives you forward and nothing is impossible.

Answer These Questions About Your Experience With Focus

- Have you ever experienced a time when you were utterly and completely focused?
- When you were in the state of focus, what did it feel like?

- What thoughts did you think while you were focused?
- How did you feel as you attacked your task with laser focus?
- What was going through your head when you were focused?
- How can you tell when you are about to get really focused?
- How do you feel after you've been in "the zone" or a state of intense focus?
- When you are focused, what kinds of things break your focus or concentration?
- What causes you to go from a state of focus to inactivity or procrastination?
- In your day-to-day life, what are the biggest distractions that keep you from staying focused when you try?

Write down your answers to all the questions on a sheet of paper right now. In order to focus better you must know two things:

1. What does focus feel like for me?
2. What keeps me from focusing?

After you have answered the previous questions, the answers to these two questions will become very clear. Take time to understand your focus profile so that you can better assess yourself as you learn the Fearsome Focus process. Once you've gone through the process with one task, go back and ask yourself the questions again. Notice the difference that going through this system makes to your outcome.

Now let's learn Fearsome Focus. The formula for creating Fearsome Focus looks like this:

1. Clearly define what you'll focus your effort on.
2. Define the action steps necessary to accomplish the project.
3. Surround yourself with the necessary tools and stimuli related directly to what you'll be focusing on.

4. Do not allow distractions to divert your attention.
5. Launch into the project.
6. Evaluate the success of your effort frequently by consulting your action steps and immediately reengaging.
7. If you are confronted with a physical or mental distraction, simply acknowledge the distraction, do what is necessary to dismiss or remove it, and then instantly reengage.
8. Continue until all action steps are complete.
9. Acknowledge completion and relax.

The formula works because you are always able to bring yourself back on track, and not bringing yourself back on track is the biggest mistake you'll make. It is inevitable in any time of focus that other stimuli will impact your concentration. The interruption can come in the form of an errant or persistent thought or a more obvious event like a co-worker dropping in.

It isn't the interruption itself that kills focus; it is the lack of immediate return to the action that destroys the outcome. Watch two boxers in a ring: Each is concentrating on a game plan and his interaction with his opponent. When a boxer gets hit, he focuses on covering up, moving, and hitting back. It is only when his focus and rhythm break that he starts getting hit hard and ultimately may lose.

The Fearsome Focus Process

Clearly Define What You'll Focus Your Effort On

You must be able to clearly define what you'll be focusing your effort on in order to give it your full attention. By being clear in your intent and definition, you become able to narrow your attention to the most important details. Clear definition also allows you to quickly check your progress to insure that you remain on track. Saying "I'm going to do the top three projects on my to do list in the next three hours" will not be nearly as effective in developing focus as saying "I'm going to write the new compensation plan for the sales team in the next 45 minutes."

Define the Action Steps Necessary to Accomplish the Project

Break your project down into manageable steps so that you can focus your attention on completing each step. By knowing what you are doing and what you'll accomplish next you are able to easily follow the plan. You are also mentally checking off tasks that have been accomplished each time you complete a step. Defining action steps insures proper and speedy completion of the project and allows you to return to your focused state quickly if you are sidetracked.

Surround Yourself with Tools and Stimuli Related to Your Focus

Any time you don't have something you need to complete a task, you create a break in focus. Spend a moment as you line out your steps to identify which tools you'll need, and then acquire them. You should also determine whether additional stimuli or other material will be necessary. If you are creating a compensation plan, you may need books, financial reports, or a current sales magazine that has a unique idea for compensation plans; these may stimulate some ideas you will want to incorporate into your plan.

Do Not Allow Distractions to Divert Your Attention

Outside distractions, like physical interruptions, are by far the most obvious focus killers that you'll encounter, but the biggest offenders are the random thoughts and internal distractions that we allow to divert our attention.

If you are working in an office, close the door, put a sign on your cube, or remove yourself from the location where you are likely to be disturbed. Be sure to let the people who are likely to disturb you know that you are not to be bothered for a defined length of time. Give specific instructions about what constitutes an emergency, so that people know exactly what they can interrupt you for.

Don't forget to remove or minimize the biggest focus killers: cell phones, e-mail, instant messages, pagers, and your BlackBerry.

Launch into the Project

Believe it or not, not taking a decisive action to begin keeps many people from focusing. Once you've followed the previous steps, you must launch into the project with the intention of making rapid progress.

Focus is a physical and mental process. Your body physiology will support your effort to focus. As you gain more experience with finding your focus you'll notice that there is a specific way you feel when you hit your stride, when you are focused. Once you know what that feeling is, you can more quickly recreate it, and you'll also have the immediate feedback that lets you know you are in your zone.

Evaluate Your Success Frequently by Consulting Your Action Steps and Immediately Reengaging

The more experience you gain with focus, the easier and more automatic checking your progress will become. The ability to focus intensely and to maintain your focus is supported by being able to see progress even when it appears to be minimal. As long as your mind recognizes positive achievements, it will support moving the process forward no matter how hard it seems. Once you get off-track or can no longer see success, your brain will present you with many more distractions that will pull your focus away.

When Confronted with Physical or Mental Distractions, Acknowledge Them, Do What Is Necessary to Dismiss or Remove Them, and Instantly Reengage

Instant reengagement is your Fearsome Focus secret weapon. Whenever you are distracted, do not spend any time thinking or talking about how focused you were. Simply acknowledge the distraction, dismiss it or deal with it if necessary, then dismiss it.

Because internally generated distractions can be the most destructive, the moment you catch yourself wandering with a thought, stop. Acknowledge that there was an attempt to pull your focus away, then renew your focus by assessing where you are in your process and reengage. The process is the same for external distractions: dismiss them, or deal with them, dismiss them, and then instantly reengage.

Continue until All Action Steps Are Complete

Do not allow your focus to change unless there is some compelling reason that you cannot continue. Be methodical in your approach. Follow your action steps, evaluate, reengage, and repeat until you've completed your task.

Acknowledge Completion and Relax

Focus is an intense effort that achieves incredible outcomes, but focus can't last forever. Once you've completed your project, mentally acknowledge that you've been successful, your task is complete or has come to a predetermined end, and you can now relax your focus.

By relaxing your focus, you allow your brain and your body to release built-up stress. Take a few deep breaths, take a quick walk, get a drink of water—do something to put a little mental space between your last project and your next. This becomes even more important if the next project will require you to focus intensely again.

Focus is a skill that is improved with practice. You should regularly practice focus in different areas of your life. The more and better you can focus, the more quickly and efficiently you can get anything done.

A Few Tips for Focus Success

- Schedule specific times that you focus; try to make them the same every day or week. Think about any other routine you have; if you are in the habit of doing it, it is nearly automatic. Focus responds very much the same way to predictable times.
- Create an environment that supports your focus, and focus in that environment consistently. Train your brain and body to react in a predictable way based on external circumstances or stimuli.
- Expand your ability to concentrate. Concentration is another form of focus. By expanding your ability to concentrate you'll expand your ability to focus. You'll simply apply the power of concentration on focus. The better you concentrate, the less internal interruptions you'll have.

Throughout this book you'll be presented with many opportunities to focus for one hour at a time. Your ability to create change in your life or your business is directly related to your ability to create intense focus. To help you get started, let's go through the first one-hour action plan that you can use to create Fearsome Focus.

One Hour Action Plan

What specifically do I want to accomplish?

Create Fearsome Focus

What specifically am I going to do to identify the first area of focus?

- Evaluate the areas of my company that I most want to improve and develop a complete plan with action steps to improve it.
- Evaluate the information I collected from the previous questions and work through the answers to fully understand why I'm under–taking this action and what I must do to be successful.
- List the specific steps that are necessary to achieve the desired result.
- Add deadlines to each step.
- Note who will be involved in or responsible for each step if others are to be involved.
- Allocate and schedule the time for this action plan and associated steps to be implemented.
- How will you define success so you know that you've been successful?
- What is the one action step you can take this very moment that will initiate this action plan?

How to
Think Critically

Critical thinking is a skill that is mandatory for you to learn, understand, and employ in order to transform your business or life in an hour a week. Critical thinking gives you a solid foundation for identifying problems and developing powerful solutions to those problems.

What Is Critical Thinking?

Many people don't really know what it means to think critically. Critical thinking is often misinterpreted as thinking something negative or critical about an idea, and nothing could be further from the truth.

Critical thinking is the process of evaluating information, ideas, and situations in order to come to the most reasonable and justifiable decision on the issue. Let me give you an example of critical thinking in action.

You have probably heard that you lose 90 percent of your body heat through your head. In fact, you've likely repeated that idea without even thinking it through. We'll apply very simple critical thinking to the idea and see if it holds up.

Questions to Ask

1. What percentage of the human body is the head?
2. Is it possible to lose such a large proportion of body heat through a part that represents a relatively small percentage of the total body?
3. Is there some reason that the head releases heat at a rate higher than the combined rest of the body?
4. If the answer to statement number 3 is yes, then I should be able to wear nothing but a stocking cap and stay warm. Is that possible?

Analysis

Simple deduction in this case shows that it is unlikely that we lose 90 percent of body heat through the head. A possible alternative is that, when the rest of the body is covered but the head is not, we lose 90 percent of the heat that is escaping through our head. If we are still unsure, simple testing would prove or disprove the theory. If we could retain 90 percent of our body heat by wearing only a hat, then we should be able to stand in a walk-in freezer comfortably dressed in nothing but a hat. By stripping down to nothing but a stocking cap and stepping into the freezer, we'd be able to tell in moments whether or not the statement were true.

I use a rather ludicrous example because every day in our business and personal lives we are faced with equally questionable opportunities. We have to make a decision about whether or not to take action based on the information we receive. If we don't have a strong critical thinking process in place, we will miss great opportunities and fall prey to many ideas that could easily be disproved.

In our daily lives and businesses, the Internet and exposure to messages from the media with their own agenda have increased the need for regular critical thinking. Think about the number of urban myths that have been forwarded to you via e-mail or the ideas that are presented as fact on web pages. There is even a whole web site with thousands of entries (www.snopes.com) that is devoted to dispelling urban myths and rumors. Also consider the amount of information you receive from television, radio, newspapers, and direct mail outlets that have very specific agendas and premises, which may or may not be completely factual.

Critical thinking is not a hard process, but it does require that we actually stop and think. The messages that slip past our critical thinking filters are often designed to do exactly that. The information is presented in such a way that, when it is encountered, it won't be evaluated, it will just be accepted as truth or fact. Some techniques used to create messages that persuade are: presentation of information as a fact; presentation of information as an interesting story told in context of a verifiable event (for example, a story of extreme sadness and hope coming out of a major natural disaster for the purpose of raising money, but which is really a combination of abstracted incidents from many disasters). Other techniques include outright lying, leaving out key pieces of information and allowing you to draw an implied conclusion, and many more.

I didn't write this chapter to make you paranoid or feel like you need to think critically about every action you take. The point is simply to let you know that if you get a message that seems suspect or too good to be true, you may want to think about it. I'm also presenting the information so that you can make better and more informed decisions based on sound reasoning that will allow you to move forward quickly and profitably.

How to Think Critically

The critical thinking process is not hard; it simply requires that we ask questions and validate the answers we receive. The power of critical thinking is in the original questions and the follow-up questions we ask. The better and more complete the information we receive, the more likely we are to make a correct decision about an event.

The steps to critical thinking are:

1. Acknowledge that you are a critical thinker and apply the skills regularly.
2. Understand the blocks to critical thinking and avoid them.
3. Listen for and understand arguments.
4. Evaluate the legitimacy of the evidence.
5. Evaluate the case.

Acknowledge that You Are a Critical Thinker and Apply the Skills Regularly

Critical thinking does not remove choice or emotion; it simply gives you a way of determining what the appropriate decision is even when you are being influenced heavily by your emotions. By practicing critical thinking you can make better decisions in highly charged environments. Work on developing the key attributes of a critical thinker every day and you'll quickly find yourself making better decisions.

The key attributes demonstrated by the critical thinker are intellectual flexibility, curiosity, reasonable skepticism, independent mind, and willingness to explore. Let's look at each a little more closely.

Intellectual flexibility is the ability and willingness to consider multiple ideas and viewpoints and weigh them rationally for the purpose of coming to a conclusion, even when the conclusion may be different from your current beliefs. In order to think critically you have to be willing to accept that there may be an idea or solution different from your own. You must also be willing to try on the new idea for fit even when it impacts a strongly held belief. If you can temporarily suspend your belief, you can give an idea a much more thorough evaluation.

Curiosity gives us the ability to ask more and better questions. The more curious we are about a subject and the more we approach it with an attitude of learning or exploring, the more information we'll receive. Be specific in your questioning and you'll get better answers.

Having an independent mind means being able not to allow social pressure or outside influences to color your decision-making process. Social pressure and group-think are powerful compliance tools, but they are also strong indicators that significant critical thinking is required. Consider what the group is saying and what they want, but look at the issues rationally and independently in order to decide whether the group is right. Most social pressure and group-think revolve around generalities rather than specifics. Drill down to the specifics and determine if they support the group ideology.

Finally, willingness to explore means having the courage to discipline yourself to always look for better ideas. In my life and business, my willingness to explore has led to more breakthroughs and new opportunities than any other single thing. By looking in unexpected places for solutions, or by questioning norms, you'll always find new possibilities. Discipline allows you to put in the required effort and study necessary to making good judgments.

Understand the Blocks to Critical Thinking and Avoid Them

The language used to present an argument can conceal the truth, mislead, or confuse us. We must listen carefully to what is being said and clarify the language. Beliefs and prejudices are blocks to critical thinking; you must temporarily suspend belief and prejudice in order to fully explore the possibility of the situation. Challenge the old idea of "it's always been done this way."

The use of numbers and data is also a block used by those who would have us not think critically. It is imperative that you question data and understand the methodology used to develop the numbers. Was a statistically viable sample used to come up with the information? What were the specific questions asked and answered that led to this conclusion? Of all the techniques of deception and confusion, numbers and data are the easiest to use to get us to make snap judgments. If 9 out of 10 people believe something, then it must be true, right? Well, it depends on who those 9 out of 10 people are and what they were asked. Don't let ideas supported primarily by numbers slip past you. Question them in more detail if they are designed to sway a belief you hold or decision you've made. If they are real and correct and impact your belief, then be willing to change.

Listen for and Understand Arguments

The word argument is often used in place of quarrel or disagreement. To the critical thinker, argument is used to present reasons to support a conclusion. Listen for words or phrases such as "leading to the conclusion," because, so, and for. Those words or phrases prior to a conclusion typically indicate that the previous information was the justification for the decision.

Arguments can be broken down into two categories, inductive and deductive. In a deductive argument B can necessarily be inferred from A. So, if all pilots can fly a plane and Tim is a pilot, it follows that he can fly a plane.

Inductive arguments are not black and white. They do not reach their conclusions by necessity; they seek to prove their arguments with reasonable grounds for the conclusion. No matter how reasonable the grounds, they will never prove the conclusion with absolute certainty. When you are seeking a conclusion to an inductive argument, you must assess degrees of probability rather than right or wrong, as well as the degree to which elements leading to the conclusion are all true. If the premise of the argument is true, it leads to a higher likelihood that the conclusion is also correct if the premise was properly interpreted.

Evaluate the Legitimacy of the Evidence

In order to come to a good conclusion it is mandatory that you evaluate the evidence that is being used to support the conclusion. Evidence is usually presented in terms of facts found in books or other publications, first-hand experience of an individual, or published studies and research.

As I pointed out earlier about numbers, it is imperative that you question the validity of the information you are receiving. If the information is coming from a person, does he have the requisite qualifications and experience to make such a statement or decision? Does he have any reason to spin the information or demonstrate another bias? Does he have a track record of accuracy?

When making a decision, be sure that you are relying on information that is accurate, honest, and complete. Leading people to incorrect conclusions by omission is still lying. Evaluating evidence is one of the most time-consuming tasks when thinking critically.

Evaluate the Case

Evaluating the sum total of the information is the process that will allow you to decide what to believe or what course of action to follow in a particular situation. You have to ask yourself if the assumptions are correct, whether they are known to be true, or if the evidence suggests that it is reasonable to accept the assumption without further exploration.

You must further ask if there is sufficient relevant information to support the reasoning that led to the conclusion. When you weight the evidence to support or disprove an argument, the more validity the sources of contradictory or supporting evidence have, the stronger the weight of the argument.

Finally, you have to ask if the argument is complete. Are you making a decision based on all the facts or are some facts missing? If there are missing facts, then you must go back and research further to establish full factual information before you make a final decision.

Critical thinking will allow you to make better decisions faster and will help remove the emotional component associated with snap decisions.

Critical thinking can happen very quickly or it may take time, depending on the severity of the decision and the amount of information you have at hand when you make it. When confronted with a requirement to make a snap decision, ineffective thinkers base their decision on their emotions alone; critical thinkers follow a process to insure the highest probability of making the correct decision. If after you've followed the critical thinking process your gut tells you something is missing, it probably is. Go back over your evidence, look at the argument closely, and follow the critical thinking steps again until you have the correct decision.

Ultimately putting the decision into action is the final test of the conclusion. If when you test you gather more feedback or information, be flexible enough to know when to modify your decision. What is conclusively true today may not be true tomorrow, because of additional information or circumstances that didn't exist before. Almost everything that was held to be true 500 years ago has been proven incorrect by the information and understanding we have today. Remain flexible, think critically, and apply actively. That is the key to creating successful solutions.

CHAPTER

How to Think Creatively

In terms of transforming your life or business, being able to think creatively is a skill that will serve you well for your whole career. Creative thinking is often misinterpreted to mean pushing the rules. It is also often thought of in the artistic sense. While either of these definitions could work in some cases, I define creative thinking this way: Creative thinking is the ability to connect the seemingly unconnected to create a new possibility.

Some people believe creative thinking is hard. In reality it isn't; we do it spontaneously and naturally every day. Virtually every one of us has good ideas when we are thinking about something. Creative thinking happens because you use a creative thinking process and you focus time on it. Creative thinking is a skill that can be effectively developed to make you wildly effective.

One of the first things I do with new clients is take them through a series of creative thinking exercises. I want their minds prepared to think expansively, I want them thinking about possibilities, and I want them to know that virtually anyone can think creatively.

Try this exercise right now.

Encountering Einstein

Albert Einstein is considered one of the brightest and best thinkers in recent history. If you could have a moment of his thoughts and wisdom, would you be able to find a nugget of wisdom that you could use or apply? Remember, Einstein was working as a lowly patent clerk when he developed the theory of relativity. He made some wild connections—you can too.

Read the following paragraphs in full first, then do the exercises. Before you start, I want you to pick one simple problem for which you'd like to have alternative solution. Don't make it a save-the-world problem, just something that you are stuck on and would like some new ideas about.

First Exercise

I want you to take a deep breath through your nose, pull it all the way down to your hips, expand your ribs and stomach as you do it, hold it for a couple of seconds, then let it out. Do it again. Close your eyes and imagine you are walking down the beach, the sun is shining, there is a warm breeze blowing in your face, and all your favorite scents are in the air. Really notice how things feel—the sun penetrating your muscles, the wind on your face, the wonderful smells mixing in your nose. As you walk you see a bench and decide to sit down and relax. You stretch your legs out in front of you and spread your arms along the back of the bench; you tilt your head and let it rest on the back of the bench. As you relax, you realize that someone is sitting next to you.

You look over and realize that the stranger looks vaguely familiar and, just as you realize it is Albert Einstein, he says "hello." Mr. Einstein continues: "I noticed a puzzled look on your face, as if you were pon-

dering a question. Would you tell me what it was that you were thinking about?"

As you continue to relax, ask Professor Einstein your question. Notice
his look as he thinks about what you asked. Notice how he's already for-
mulated an answer, or several, and he begins to blurt them out. Pay attention to what he says; listen for the metaphors, the comparisons, or the
outright answers. Once he's finished, thank him, open your eyes, and write
down all of his answers in the notebook you are carrying.

If you have a hard time remembering what to do, simply read this
into a recorder and play it back. Read it in a slow, moderated voice so
you have time to take each action before the next one comes. After
you've completed the exercise, throughout that day, when a new idea
related to your question comes up, write it down. By the end of the exercise and the end of the day, you'll have many new solutions to your
problem; I guarantee it.

I want you to ask yourself this important question. Are you *not* doing
this exercise because you feel embarrassed or uncomfortable? Are you not
doing it because you don't believe in these kinds of silly little games?
Whatever your excuse is, I'm going to respectfully ask that you suspend
disbelief for a moment and simply go through the process.

Here is why the process works. When you are able to see something
through someone else's eyes, you'll have a different view. By asking yourself to frame your answers in someone else's voice and ideology you'll
come up with new ideas. Are you channeling Einstein? Of course you are
not; you are simply giving your brain permission to work outside the normal set of boundaries and structures that you use to keep it reigned in.

Information and stimulus are the keys to developing creative thinking
and ideas. If you only surround yourself with the same people and information each time you set out to solve a problem, you'll rarely get new answers to old problems. You have to feed your mind more new information
from which to draw conclusions or make decisions.

Creative Stimulus

Better questions are one of the best keys to new ideas and new thoughts. Ask questions like:

- What would happen if?
- What if we didn't?
- What if we did?
- Who could solve this problem?
- What is one thing that would never work and why?
- What is the most bizarre idea you can think of as it relates to the challenge at hand?
- How would we solve this problem if we had all the money in the world to focus on it?
- How would we solve this problem if our very lives depended on it?
- If I could wave a magic wand and fix this problem, what would happen?

Stimulus can come in many other forms. By collecting related and unrelated thoughts and ideas, we can start combining them to come up with unique possibilities.

Second Exercise

Here is an interesting exercise you can try with a problem you are facing. It takes less than an hour and is very powerful. Again, some of you who are reading this will feel uncomfortable with this kind of process. Remember, the idea is to break out of your old habits and thinking styles and come up with new possibilities.

Before you start thinking about the problem, gather a bunch of magazines—trade magazines, business magazines, sports magazines, newspapers, car magazines—as many unrelated publications as you can reasonably get your hands on.

Next, I want you to write down your problem on top of a flip chart page or on top of a white board. Write your question out so it is clearly defined. Remember clearly defined problems are fast attractors of powerful solutions.

Now, look at the question and start going through the magazines. Whenever you see something that is interesting to you, stop, cut out that picture or tear out the page and tape it to the flip chart sheet. If it reminds you of the problem, cut it out; if it is interesting, cut it out; if it is a solution to the problem, cut it out. Once you've filled your flip chart page with images and ideas, stop for a moment.

Take a look at the stimulus sheet where your problem is written down. Look at all the ideas. On a separate page, write down how each piece of paper taped to the sheet applies to the problem. Begin looking at the ideas that are emerging and start narrowing them down to usable and workable ideas or possibilities.

You'll be amazed at the result of following this process. You are freeing your mind and giving it the ability to make connections. Those connections are vital. Current brain research has conclusively proven that, when exposed to more stimuli, our brains react by making more connections between the different areas of the brain by sending more synapses through the dendrites that connect them. You have to give your brain room to grow and experience new things or it simply will not. In 1993, Dean Keith Simonton of the University of California–Davis reported on a study of 2,036 scientists throughout history (*Newsweek*, June 28). It was discovered that most highly respected scientists produced not only more great works than their scientific peers, but also more poor ones. But, because they were focused on producing, they produced.

Forget about science for a moment. A .500 hitter in baseball is a legend and even he missed half the opportunities he had to hit, but the possibility of missing didn't keep him from swinging. Take some chances—swing at the opportunities that are presented.

Spend Your Hour Creatively

Sometimes the best thing to stimulate creative thinking is to do something different. As we'll discuss throughout the rest of the book, disengaging briefly and expanding your horizons can give your brain an opportunity to make connections subconsciously that can then bubble to the surface. Here are a few ideas for spending your hour creatively.

- Go for a walk or run.
- Paint a picture.
- Write a poem.
- Visit a gallery.
- Visit someone in a hospital.
- Go to the park.
- Talk to someone from another culture.
- Eat an ethnic meal you've never had before.
- Watch a non-American television station.
- Read a magazine you'd never read.
- Count the steps from your office to wherever you walk.
- Make a prank call to your spouse, friend, or significant other.
- Eat a lollipop and count how many licks it takes to finish it.
- Buy Roger Von Oech Creative Whack Pack and follow the suggestions on one of the cards.
- Get a psychic reading.

Just do something different, broaden your horizons, and you'll broaden your ability to think creatively. The wonderful thing about creative thinking is that everyone values a creative thinker. Your value will go up as your ability to think creatively increases. The other great thing is that your brain will reward you by making more and better connections the moment you begin to practice creative thinking.

I can't stress enough how important this hour will be to you for the rest of your life. The hours you invest now will be paid back over and over again.

Warning

Most of you will not attempt even one exercise in this chapter. Do not let your fear of feeling uncomfortable hold you back. Make this an opportunity to express yourself in a way that you never have before.

One Last Exercise

For those of you who've read this far and the previous exercises were too much, do the following. Go to the local toy store and buy a giant tub of Legos. Go ahead, throw in the Lego plane and pirate ship just for fun. Hide someplace where no one can see you and build a model of your problem. Make it as big and complex as it needs to be. Then, regularly come back to it and build solutions. Even the most creatively adverse can do this exercise. Once you've done it, try the exercise with your staff. Have them build a model of the organization and explain why they built it the way they did. You'll be amazed at the insights—but don't take my word for it. Build it and the ideas will come!

Crazy Ideas into Action

The last thing you have to do when thinking creatively is bring everything back to a workable solution. You must take the best ideas and polish them. You must apply critical thinking in order to adapt them into the perfect solution. Remember, creative thinking is there to dislodge the solution.

Critical thinking allows you to give it structure and substance. Apply logic and process to make the creative ideas into workable plans.

One-Hour Action Plan

What Specifically Do I Want to Accomplish?

Think creatively.

What Specifically Am I Going to Do to Think Creatively Today?

- Identify a creativity exercise that you can do and identify a problem you'd like to apply it to.
- Evaluate the information collected from the previous questions and exercises and work through the answers to fully understand which ideas need to be cultivated and fine-tuned for implementation.
- Apply logic and critical thinking to develop a plan to implement the solution.
- List the specific steps that are necessary to achieve the desired result.
- Add deadlines to each step.
- Note who will be involved in or responsible for each step if others are to be involved.
- Allocate and schedule time for this action plan and associated steps to be implemented.
- How will you define success so we know that you've been successful?
- What is the one action step you can take this moment that will initiate this action plan?

Personal Hour 1— Set the Stage

Often attempts to create personal or business change fail because we don't adequately set ourselves up for success. In this first hour we are going to set the stage to create success with the change we will create over the coming hours.

Clearly defining your outcome is the most powerful step you will take in setting the stage. I want you to keep this scientific principle of action in mind. You should take no action external to your body until you've taken it first in your mind. And you can't take action mentally until you first decide what specifically you want to do.

The mind is an amazing machine that works both when you are consciously paying attention and when you are not. The ability to process information at a subconscious level is one of the things that allow us to achieve any desired result.

Start setting the stage by clearly defining your desired outcome in three steps.

Three Steps to Setting the Stage

1. *Clearly define what you want.* Saying you want to lose 20 pounds is not specific enough. Be clear in your intention. Here is a great example of clearly defining what you need to accomplish. "My intention is to achieve a healthy weight that I define as 180 pounds, by engaging in an exercise program to which I'm committing 45 minutes daily. I am achieving this goal to support my long-term health, so that I feel better when I look in the mirror, and to attract my perfect mate, who is also lean and fit."

2. *Define what specifically you'll do to create the change.* If you are going to engage in an exercise program or a savings program, write out exactly what steps you intend to take. Again, be specific. Saying you'll exercise 45 minutes a day is not nearly as powerful as saying you'll exercise 45 minutes per day beginning at 7:00 A.M. each morning, and then committing it in your calendar. By taking an action as simple as creating your plan you've already started moving the process forward, which helps insure success.

3. *Finally, determine how to measure success.* Many successes go unrealized because the person who has achieved so much doesn't realize he has actually reached his goal. He continues to pursue a goal after it has been achieved or, worse, he hampers success by going off on tangents, under the guise that he is trying different routes because others didn't work. Ask yourself this question every time you set out to achieve something new: How do I define success and how will I know when I've achieved it? What you can quantify and measure you can more easily achieve.

Three Steps to Setting the Stage Expanded

Let's walk through the three steps together here.

Step 1—Clearly Define What You Want

In Step 1, when you define specifically what you want, you must take the time to understand whether what you are setting out to accomplish is still a valid goal. All too often we continue to chase goals that were important once but are no longer valid. We tend to think that those things we never achieved in the past might still be worthy accomplishments. Maybe they would, but it is up to you to reevaluate your goals. Ask yourself the following questions in order to determine if your goal is still valid or if you need to let it go by the wayside and focus on a different goal.

- What do I get personally, emotionally, spiritually, or physically from achieving this goal?
- What specifically will happen when I achieve this goal?
- Is this the goal I should still be pursuing?
- In the bigger picture of my life, what does this do to support my overall desires?
- Am I achieving this goal for myself or to prove something to someone else (someone I knew in high school, college, or a past relationship) and if I am, is that person still important enough to me to invest this energy in proving something to him or her?
- If I'm achieving this goal for someone else, will he care, will he know when I'm successful, and is my desire to prove something to him going to be a strong enough driving factor to keep me focused on the goal?
- When I achieve this goal, will it serve as a stepping stone for creating the future I desire?
- What are my beliefs about this goal? What do I believe accomplishing this goal will bring me?
- What will happen if I don't accomplish this goal?
- What am I unwilling to do to accomplish this goal?

- What will happen if I abandon this goal forever, right now?
- And once again, ask yourself with all honesty, "Is this a goal that I still want to achieve?"

If your goal is worthy and you still feel as if you should pursue it, then attack it with ruthless vigor; if it isn't, drop it and never look back. Don't pursue goals that are not worthy of your effort; find better goals and move your life forward.

Let me share my personal experience. As you may know from my previous book, I grew up in a cult. Education was not encouraged; in fact, it was strongly encouraged that children leave school permanently by the sixth to eighth grades. I chose to stay in school, which resulted in my being excommunicated from the group and leaving home at 16 years of age.

In school I had two or three good friends but I definitely did not have the attention of the popular students. I was very nervous about anyone finding out about my home life or my growing up in a cult so I kept as much to myself as possible, though inside—I wanted to be accepted by my peers. After high school, I focused a lot of energy doing things that I thought would make me more accepted by my high-school peers. As my 10-year reunion approached, I was prepared to show all my high-school classmates how successful I had become. Once I was there, I realized that I no longer cared if I was accepted by the people whose attention I craved in high school. Their attention simply didn't matter any more. I had to reevaluate everything I considered important and understand why I was motivated to accomplish these things. As soon as I figured out that I was the only one keeping score and no one else was watching, I was able to focus on more meaningful goals at a much higher level.

Let me give you another example. I grew up in cult with a family that was very poor. When we moved from Oklahoma to Idaho, my mom, my middle brother, and my stepfather lived in a city park for three months in a tent while we saved enough money to find a house. Throughout my teenage years and early twenties, all of my financial mentors had struggled with money. I read several books about people who reached a very low ebb in their lives, and about the events that led to a change. So, from the time I was in my late teens to my late twenties, I struggled with money. I didn't get as much as I deserved, I never met my financial goals, and I was always looking at the low points, wondering how much lower they had to be before I could earn my rags to riches story.

Then one day I started evaluating the goals I had set. I looked at them in comparison to my beliefs and my past examples. The moment I did that, things began to change for me. By simply evaluating the reasons I was doing what I was doing, I created a whole new opportunity. Literally within a year, things began to turn around. My businesses became more successful, I made more money, and I too became successful. My final hurdle was worrying about how those closest to me, who were not as financially successful, would feel about me. Once I realized that their goals were not my goals and that these people were my biggest fans, I achieved my best level ever and have stayed there since.

Step 2—*Define Specifically What You Will Do to Create the Change*

This may well be the step that ultimately determines your success or failure; it is vital that you carefully follow the instructions in this step. Harvey Mackay, author of *Swim with the Sharks without Being Eaten Alive*, says: "Goals are dreams with deadlines." That is true, but only partially. Many people have too many dreams with missed deadlines because they didn't create a plan for achieving their goals. Simply saying you want something and setting a deadline and even taking some action is not enough. You need to have an Achievement Action Plan™.

Grab a blank sheet of paper and write down the following questions and your corresponding answers. (You can download a printable, fill-in-the-blank copy of this form, free, at www.powerofanhour.com.)

ACHIEVEMENT ACTION PLAN

What do I specifically intend to accomplish and what is the deadline for my accomplishment?

What does accomplishing this goal mean to me?

What are the three to five major components of accomplishment?

What are the exact steps that must be taken to achieve each of the three to five major components above, and what are the deadlines associated with each step?

How much time am I willing to invest each week in achieving this goal, and is my overall timeline still accurate based on that investment? (If it isn't, you must either adjust your time each week or your deadline.)

Who else and/or what else must be involved for me to create this goal?

What is one step I can take immediately after completing this form to initiate action that physically, mentally, and actually gets the project started?

How specifically will I know that I've been successful in this endeavor?

Step 3—Determine How You'll Know You've Been Successful

The fastest way to create change that is never completed is by not knowing when to stop. I want you to take a look back at all the goals you've set out to accomplish and see which ones you are still working on and which you've already completed.

What happens is that we set out to create change and our efforts become a habit and we forget to stop doing whatever action we were taking. The problem is that we never truly experience the feeling of success that comes with a completed project. The other problem is that we often sabotage our success by continuing to try and find other things to work on that move our efforts forward.

There is an old saying that goes like this: What gets measured gets done. I'd add to that: What gets measured gets done as long as we know specifically what we are measuring.

Before you set out to create any significant change or to achieve any meaningful goal, be sure you've walked through all three steps and completed an Achievement Action Plan. If you'll take this one simple step before you set out to accomplish any goal, you'll accomplish every goal you decide is worthy of your effort.

Personal Hour 2— Identify the Blocks

We all have blocks that prevent us from achieving the goals we set in our personal life or business. The problem is that many times we either don't see them or won't acknowledge them for what they are. I've seen numerous businesses, executives, and individuals transformed by finally identifying what blocks were holding them back from real success. Of course, just identifying the blocks alone is not enough. You must take action, but identification is the first step.

I recently worked with a company owned by a husband-and-wife team. The husband had left a reasonably lucrative career in the same field in order to realize his dream of owning a business. The business grew, and soon his wife quit her job and the couple started working in the business together. Things began to change. The woman was resentful of her husband's control in the business; she didn't want him giving her orders or measuring her daily activity. The man felt that his wife was not contributing enough. But neither recognized what was happening until I had them go through the exercise given later in this chapter.

It is vital that you identify your blocks and where they exist in order to be effective. The husband and wife were having problems at home that spilled over from the resentment at work. There is no way to disconnect home and work because you are the same person whether at home or at work. Blocks that result in unhappiness or lack of success in one area are carried into our other relationships and activities.

Identifying Blocks

There are four things we all want in life that we don't like to admit in polite company. They are money, fame, sex, and power. Now bear with me before you throw the book down in disgust and say you don't want all of those things. By simply framing the most common desires we all have in a very basic way, we will be more able to see what the blocks are. I dare you to frame whatever you want to accomplish in a basic way, then see if you don't discover many beliefs about your desire you didn't even know you had.

When I say most of us want money, you may have been programmed to say no. You may have been taught that money is the root of all evil, (not what the bible says, by the way) or you may say that you don't want too much money (modesty). Let me give you a personal example. I was afraid to admit for a long time that I wanted to be rich. When I broke my feelings down to the most basic level, I discovered I was worried that my mom or brothers might feel bad if I had more money than they did. The moment I understood what held me back, I was able to quickly and easily reframe my concern and overcome the obstacle. In my case, the reframe was simply acknowledging that, when I was able to make all the money I wanted, I'd be able to help my family in ways I never could before and certainly in ways no one ever had before.

By reframing, I more easily identified my beliefs about money that were holding me back and keeping me from having all I wanted. That realization and change happened in a matter of minutes when I finally started focusing on my block.

Often, blocks show up as resistance to change or accomplishment. You intend to accomplish something but every time you set out to do it you run into some resistance. Resistance is insidious and can take many forms.

Procrastination

Procrastination is a common form of resistance. You know something needs to be addressed in order to move forward, but it is easier to simply procrastinate rather than take action. While you procrastinate, your block gets stronger and stronger and your procrastination reinforces your resolve not to take action.

Ambivalence

Ambivalence is the coexistence of two opposing opinions, or indecision on which course of action to follow. You know you should diet and exercise in order to be healthier, yet you know your grandfather never exercised and lived to be 100. You don't know if exercise matters and so you take no action.

Have to or Should Do

The most important question you can ask yourself about "have to" or "should do" is "What would happen if I didn't?" All too often we use "have to" and "should do" to effectively create blocks for real change. We set up a belief that if "step X" doesn't happen first we can't move to the next level. Or worse, we believe something should be done first without having any real evidence that we are making the right decision. By simply considering the outcome if a certain action is not taken, often the consequences aren't as severe as believed or another, better solution is realized.

Excuses and Justifications

Excuses are another form of resistance that causes blocks to remain unchanged. We all have a personal dialog, complete with excuses and justifications, for not doing what we need to do in order to move forward. It's much easier to look at the block while making excuses and justifications for not taking any action. Excuses and justifications allow us to feel better about not taking action, but they only make the block bigger and harder to change.

Giving Up

By far the most common form of resistance is simply giving up. By giving up on important goals in our lives we create a new block that says, "I'm feeling resistance, so the best thing to do is quit." By reinforcing failure through giving up, you build stronger blocks. The urge to give up without having tried is easy because we use past experiences to reinforce quitting.

Identifying Blocks Exercise

In order to change your life, you have to look closely at what blocks are holding you back. It is imperative to evaluate every area of your life and prioritize which blocks need to be overcome first. In Chapter 7 we'll talk about what to do in order to create powerful action that allows you to overcome the blocks, but in this Power Hour we want to remain focused on identification.

Let's look at the most common areas of life where blocks usually appear. It is important to thoroughly assess your life because each block impacts other areas of it. The faster you can remove blocks, the faster you'll achieve results in all life areas. Ask yourself, as you look at the following list, "In which areas do I feel resistance even though I know I must create change in order to move forward?" Write down where you have a block or feel resistance. Be as concise as possible.

Business

- Controlled direction
- Sales
- Marketing and advertising
- Finance
- Operations
- Employees
- Growth
- Profitability

Career

- My position
- My supervisor
- My employees
- My compensation
- My workload
- My company
- My level of success
- My coworkers
- My accomplishments
- My promotion path

Income and Financial Situation

- My earnings
- My spouse or significant other's earnings
- My savings
- My credit
- My current financial position
- My net worth
- My retirement
- My investments

Business Relationships

- My vendors
- My partners
- My clients
- My industry
- My involved family members

Personal Relationships

- My friends
- My acquaintances
- My extended family
- My immediate family
- My physician
- My accountant
- My broker

Intimate Relationships

- My spouse or significant other
- My sex life
- My living arrangement
- My relationship
- My relationship with myself

Health

- My physical well-being
- My mental well-being
- My weight
- My diet
- My exercise routine
- My proactive health maintenance

Education

- My education level
- My job or career skills level
- My beliefs about education

Self-Worth

- My self-esteem
- My worthiness
- My place in the world around me

Spirituality

- My definition of spirituality
- My spiritual beliefs
- My spiritual leaders
- My spiritual practice
- My connectedness to the world around me

While the categories tend to be quite broad, they cover, in my experience, every area of life that ultimately supports or undermines your attempts to create change rapidly. Go back down the list, and add a little more detail to each category by asking the following questions:

- In which of these areas do I experience resistance to change?
- What specifically needs to change in my life in order for me to achieve the goals I've set for myself in each area?
- How does my resistance manifest itself, in procrastination, ambivalence, have to or should do, excuses and justifications, giving up, or all of the above?
- If I focused on changing one of these blocks today, which would have the most universal impact throughout my life? How?
- As I read through this exercise, what was the excuse or resistance I first used for not doing the exercise immediately?
- Recognizing that, what block could I change right now that would have the most universal impact through my life?

I wrote this book by combining two different topics, business and personal development, because they are so interconnected. Manifestations of blocks in one area, inevitably lead to some conflict or block in the other. Nearly every business I work with ultimately has to address personal blocks in order to create the business change needed to achieve success.

Recently I spoke with a CEO who wanted to hire my company. He started the conversation by telling me he would dictate what we'd do for him and how. I asked him why he thought he needed outside help. He said he "needed new ideas and tactics to grow." In just a brief conversation, we identified one block that would have to be addressed in order for him to move forward—his need to be in control at any cost. Upon further conversation I decided that we would not be a good fit for him because he refused to accept that there might be ideas he hadn't considered or didn't understand, which might work for him but would require him to step out of his comfort zone.

Before you move on to the next chapter, which is about taking action to create change, go through the One-Hour Action Plan right now. If you'll take time to honestly assess your blocks you'll be able to use the rest of this book much more effectively in order to achieve successful transformation.

One-Hour Action Plan

What Do I Want to Accomplish?

Identify the blocks in every area of my life and business.

What Specifically Am I Going to Do To Reinvent Myself or an Area of My Life or Career?

- Specifically define the blocks that you identified above.
- Evaluate the information collected from the previous questions and work through the answers to fully understand why you are blocked in this area.
- List the specific areas of your life and business that are impacted by your identified blocks.

- Add deadlines for taking action to remove the blocks.
- Note who will be involved in or responsible for each step if others are to be involved.
- Allocate and schedule the time for this action plan and associated steps to be implemented.
- How will success be defined so you know when you've been successful?
- Define what removing these blocks allows you to do that you are not doing now.

Read Chapter 7 to learn how to take positive action that will allow you to overcome your blocks.

Your ability to quickly identify and overcome the blocks in your business or life will dictate how quickly you can achieve success. I recommend going through this exercise at least once a quarter if not once a month to maximize your success.

Personal Hour 3—Destroy the Blocks

In Chapter 6 you went through an exercise that helped you to identify blocks in your business or personal life. Now it is time to remove them to pave the way for successful change.

Removing blocks is really not as hard as most of us make it out to be. Clear identification of the obstacle is the first and most important step in the process. What you can clearly define you can easily change. If you haven't already gone through the process in the last chapter, I strongly recommend you go back now and do the exercise.

The second and equally important step in the process is to clearly identify what you'd like the outcome to be. Clearly defined outcomes with a plan for success result in goals achieved. That brings us to the third part of destroying obstacles: developing a road map for success.

Over the next chapters, I'll help you work through creating a road map for some of the major obstacles in your business and your career. In this chapter I will break down the process of destroying blocks so that you can apply these methods to virtually any situation in which you are blocked.

The Four-Step Block Buster Plan

- Clearly identify and describe the block you are facing.
- Define specifically the result you intend to achieve by removing the block.
- Define your plan and timeline for removing the block.
- Take action.

Clearly Identify and Describe the Block You Are Facing

To repeat: If you haven't already done the exercise in the last chapter, go back and do it now. The more specific you can be in describing what is blocking you, the easier it is to find a solution. Let me give you an example of how many conversations go and why there is rarely resolution:

> "Everything you do makes me angry!"
> "Everything you do makes me angry too."
> "Something has to change or this will never work out!"
> "You first."

It sounds funny, but can you see the futility in trying to overcome the problem that exists between the two people having this conversation? In order to have any possibility of moving forward, one of the people in the conversation has to ask better questions in order to get a quantifiable description of what needs to happen.

> "Everything you do makes me angry!"
> "Everything?"
> "Yes!"
> "Can you give me a specific example of what I do that is making you angry?"

"You refuse to respect me."

"Just so I'm clear by what you mean, can you give me an example of how I'm disrespectful?"

"You never mow the lawn or take care of the outside of the house and it is embarrassing."

"Is there anything else that I do that makes you feel disrespected?"

"Not really. I just want you to help me by cleaning up outside. I've told you a million times."

"So if I help you by cleaning up outside and mowing the lawn regularly, would you feel respected?"

"Yes, I guess so."

"Is there anything else I need to do in order not to make you feel angry with me?"

"Not that I can think of right now."

"Okay, I'll work on the lawn in an hour and get the outside cleaned up."

"Okay, Thanks."

Do you see how by asking more specific questions one person was able to narrow down what was causing the problem or the block in communication? Generalizations are rarely correct when it comes to identifying blocks. You can either clearly identify the problem in the beginning or you can solve a lot of problems that don't exist before you find the one that really does.

Here are some generalizations that we all use when it comes to creating change:

- I don't have enough time.
- It costs too much.
- It isn't my responsibility.
- I just don't want to do it.
- I'll get around to it.

- It's always been this way; it will never or can't change.
- It doesn't matter; it won't make a difference anyway.
- I've tried before, but it doesn't work.
- It will cause a fight with my spouse, family, or significant other.

You can add a few of your own best generalizations here (notice how much generalizations sound like excuses?).

Once you've narrowed down the block, write it out clearly. "I don't have enough money" is not specific or clear. "Based on my current financial needs, I have a $10,000 shortfall, which is keeping me from realizing my financial goals" is much more specific. The more specific and quantifiable you can make the block, the easier it is to come up with a solution that will destroy the block.

Define Specifically the Result You Intend to Achieve by Removing the Block

Clearly defining the block by itself is a good start, but you also have to know what you'll achieve by removing the block. You must have a worthy and compelling reason for change if you want to destroy the block that holds you back.

The person in the above example said "Based on my current financial needs, I have a $10,000 shortfall, which is keeping me from realizing my financial goals." In order to define specifically the result you intend to achieve, ask this question: "What will removing this block allow me to do and how will it move me forward?"

Staying with the example above, simply saying "It will allow me to reach my financial goals" is not specific enough. On the other hand, "By increasing my income by $10,000 per year, I'll be able to contribute monthly to my retirement plan, meet all of my monthly financial obligations, improve my credit score by being timely with my payments, and allow me to increase my savings to a full 10 percent of my income" is much more specific and therefore achievable. Add to that, "By accomplishing this goal, I'll feel more financially secure and will be able to support my family in the way I believe is important. There will be enough money so that my wife can quit her job and stay home to raise the children. I support that goal, which is one of her primary goals and one that I strongly believe in." Now you have a statement that is clear, concise, and compelling—something you can build a plan around that will stick, because you know what you need to do and what you'll achieve by doing it.

Define Your Action Plan and Timeline for Removing the Block

An action plan is the key to your long-term success in removing blocks. At the end of most of the chapters in this book there is a one-hour action plan that helps you give structure to the one hour you'll invest in jump-starting your transformation.

The keys to an effective action plan are specificity and breaking the activity down to the smallest steps so that you can create achievable goals on your way to total success.

Again, using our earlier example of the need to create an additional $10,000 in incremental income, we'll develop a plan that will allow forward motion.

Action Plan and Timeline

- Quantify how much $10,000 means per paid work hour, day, week, and month. $10,000 equals $4.80 per paid work hour, $38.46 per day, $192.30 per week, and $769.30 per month.

- Ask my boss for a $3.00 per hour raise and be prepared to settle for $2.00, which will equal $4,160.00 of the needed increase. Timeline: Ask Monday and allow one pay period before I will see the increase.
- Pay off one credit card and close the account. The current payment is $150 per month; eliminating this will amount to $1,800 in savings per year. Assuming the raise and payoff, I've now reached $5,960 of the needed increase. Timeline: Pay off the card next month.
- I've wanted to start an eBay business. I'll do this by selling my baseball card collection, which is valued at $5,000.00. Then I will invest $3,000.00 back into the business and keep $2,000 toward my $10,000 goal. I anticipate that I can realistically earn $3,000 per year buying and selling trading cards, since I currently do it as a hobby and earn about $150 per month. That gives me $8,960 toward my needed $10,000. Timeline: Two months from now I'll sell my first cards on eBay. Between now and then I'll study three books on becoming an eBay powerseller.
- Finally, I'll give up my morning espresso drink, which will save me $4.00 per day or $1,040.00 per year, giving me a total $10,000 net increase in my yearly income. Timeline: Tomorrow.

By clearly defining the plan and establishing a timeline, the block is easily defeated because each step is manageable. You now also have a roadmap for success. If you do not meet your goal, you can go back to your plan and see where you got off track. It is important to actually write these things down so you won't forget. I write my plans down in two places, always do them electronically, save them, then print and put them in my "Blockbuster Book," which I refer to regularly. The second thing I do is write the most important ones in a small notebook that I carry with me and can refer to wherever I am. Reviewing the most important efforts daily is vitally important to your success.

Take Action

Have one action step you can take immediately. It can be as simple as committing your plan to your Blockbuster Book or giving up your espresso drink the following day. By committing and taking your first action, you begin achieving your goals. Because action feels so good, you are more likely to continue.

If your actions rely on the response of another person for success (like asking for a raise), have an alternate plan if that person does not cooperate. Do not let a setback be the impetus for failure; simply replace one idea with another and keep your momentum moving forward.

One-Hour Action Plan

What Specifically Do I Want to Accomplish?

Destroy these specific blocks (Place your clearly defined block descriptions here).

What Specifically Am I Going to Do to Destroy My Blocks?

- Go through the Four-Step Block Buster Plan.
- Write out Block Buster action plan.
- List the specific steps that are necessary to achieve the desired result.
- Add deadlines to each step.
- Note who will be involved in or responsible for each step.
- Allocate and schedule the time for this action plan and associated steps to be implemented.
- How will you define success so you know you've been successful?

- What is the one action step you can take this very moment that will initiate this action plan?

Remember that speed of change and accomplishment are directly related to your ability to be clear and concise in your description of what you want to change and what you want in its place. By implementing the Four-Step Block Buster Plan, you'll be able to easily identify a way to overcome any block in an hour or less.

CHAPTER 8

Personal Hour 4— Relationships

Many experts say you can determine someone's wealth potential by averaging the wealth of their five closest friends. In reality, that is a generalization that could be applied to many endeavors. The people we choose to associate with on a regular basis will have the most significant impact on our beliefs and actions. As humans we tend to be more like people we associate with than those whom we would like to emulate but with whom we have no regular contact.

I don't think you should get rid of all your long-term relationships. However, I do believe that, in order to become more like who you want to be, you need to spend more time with and learn from those who are already there.

Taking an hour to evaluate these relationships and determine whom you'll deal with is an important hour to spend. Often it is our relationships that cost us the most time and keep us from achieving change as quickly as we might otherwise.

I want you to ask yourself right now, are your closest friends strongly supportive of the life you are creating? I don't mean supportive in words alone; I mean supportive because they are following a dream of

their own and can truly empathize with you and support you when
needed.

What I'm about to say next makes a lot of people angry, but it is the
truth whether you choose to believe it or not. Relationships need to be
categorized by their usefulness. It is possible to maintain many relationships if you understand why you are maintaining them and what they are
doing for you. Relationships also need to be a two-way street. If you are
the only giver in the relationship (unless you are doing charity work) and
the other person only takes, that is probably not a valuable relationship. In
fact, it is probably a relationship that needs to lapse.

Energy Thieves

Before I go into categorizing relationships, I want to talk to you about energy thieves. Energy thieves are people who come around only to waste
your time, who always need to share their problems with you and who always want you to support them emotionally. It is impossible to provide
support to a person who is an energy thief without giving up too much of
your own vital energy.

Energy thieves exist in all areas of our lives. You know who they are,
you can feel them start to drag you down the minute they arrive or call.
They show up as neighbors, co-workers, old friends, and in many other
guises as well. It is imperative that you identify the energy thieves early and
either exorcise them from your life or, at minimum, control their impact
by giving them only limited access.

Be aware of how much time you are spending with energy thieves and
look for ways to take back your time. The important thing to know about
these people is that they crave attention and if they are not getting it from
you, they'll get it from someone else and eventually leave you alone. There
is no value in having continued interactions with people who steal your
momentum and energy.

Categorizing Relationships

It is important to break your relationships down into categories so you can appropriately manage them. Most people will never take this one crucial step and will try to apply the same level of attention and management to all their relationships. It is virtually impossible to create the life you want while giving the same amount of attention to every relationship you have. Let's look at the most important relationship categories.

- Family
- Mutually beneficial and supportive relationships
- Long-term friends
- One-sided relationships

Let's examine the components of each category and start placing your friends into their appropriate niche.

Family

The family component is fairly obvious and also quite dangerous in terms of your ability to create the life you want. I'm a big believer in family and think that families should be able to rely on each other for support. However, at some point a little tough love may be necessary for everyone to move forward.

Because of how important family and connectedness are, family members should have easy access to you. They also need to understand that you have priorities and can't just drop everything every time they need you. The great news about most families is that this is understood, though I've seen many exceptions to the rule.

Family beliefs are the most common blocks to success. Your mother or father may have believed something like "you have to have a job with a good company to be successful," but your desire is to own your own business. Glenn Dietzel, CEO of Awakened, LLC, (www.awakentheauthorwithin.com) told me that, before he started his business, he was fearful because of his father's beliefs which included insecurity about getting in front of people and taking a risk. Once he was able to put some distance between his beliefs and his father's, he was able to become totally successful. Glenn started a business and replaced both his income as a school administrator and his wife's income in just four months.

Give your family the support they need, but give yourself some distance and create other relationships that are supportive of your own personal beliefs and desires. Don't let the power of family relationships hold you back; they are too powerful if not offset by other equally compelling relationships combined with strong desire.

Mutually Beneficial and Supportive Relationships

These relationships may include some of your long-term friends but also various people who are not long-term friends. You need to fully embrace the idea that you can have a circle of friends for mutually beneficial support who may never interact with your closest or oldest friends.

The reason you need to have some relationships in this category is that they will move your life forward in a way your other relationships can't. Often, these new friends and your closest friends won't mix because they don't have the same ideas, goals, or commitments. They often won't have had the same life experiences. You are a bridge between the two different groups, and as a bridge you often spend too much time trying to connect people. Simply recognize that the new group is separate and important and may be distinctly different from your long-term friends.

Mutually beneficial and supportive relationships need to be categorized this way for another important reason. As you move forward in your evolution, they may no longer serve the same purpose as they do today.

When I was in law enforcement I had a number of strongly beneficial and supportive relationships. When I decided to make a transition away from law enforcement, the majority of those people were no longer mutually beneficial and supportive. I couldn't support them in the same way I had in the past and my benefit to them became limited. From my perspective, most of them could not support or benefit my new direction either, so the relationships naturally ended. Of course, there were some long-term relationships that existed inside this group, people who shared similar goals and who are still among my closest friends today. If I hadn't categorized those people carefully (and in the beginning I didn't), I'd still be pulled back into an old lifestyle and many beliefs that I no longer hold important.

Since that time, I've developed more mutually supportive and beneficial relationships that support my current beliefs and allow me to move forward. There is always an ebb and flow in those relationships, and many of them end. Inevitably, there will be long-term friends who evolve from this group, and that is wonderful.

By categorizing some relationships, you have great flexibility in determining how the relationship will go and the purpose it will serve. It also makes ending the relationship easier because you were clear on your intention for the connection in the first place.

Long-Term Friends

Long-term friends are those people with whom you've been connected on a fairly intimate level for a long time or with whom you intend to stay connected for a long time. These are the people who show up at barbeques, weddings, and funerals. These are people you can call to lend a hand when you are moving your kids' swing set, or lend an ear when you need it most. They are people you care deeply about and who care deeply about you. They are also the people who, even if you don't see them for years, are still close friends the next time you see them.

Long-term friends need their own category because the way you interact with them is different; they may be closer than family in terms of access and connection. They are people who are going to be your biggest cheerleaders but not necessarily your biggest believers, because they have a hard time imagining what you are doing for themselves. They want the very best for you, but they will worry behind your back or try to be the voice of reason when they don't understand your decisions. Your new skills and transformation support won't come from this group in the beginning; it will come from your mutually beneficial and supportive relationships. In the end, once you've been successful, your long-term friends will remain your biggest cheerleaders and wonder how you did it—and they will still be your friends.

Long-term friends are important because they add the excitement to life that makes it worth living. Just be sure you are not spending so much time with them that you are pulled back into an area of complacency or old beliefs that no longer work.

One-Sided Relationships

One-sided relationships are those that take more than they give. In terms of taking up your time and challenging your progress, one-sided relationships can be devastating. The reason that one-sided relationships typically impact us negatively is our innate desire to help others. We feel guilty if we don't help.

Let me say this very plainly. There is no reason for you to feel as if you have to help someone who isn't giving you something in return, unless you simply want to provide some form of charity. And charity has limits, so you have to pick whom you'll help.

My strongest suggestion for you is to eliminate one-sided relationships immediately. Unless you can get something in return from the relationship, let it die. One-sided relationships will die a natural death because they need to be fed. Once you stop feeding them, they go away quickly. You'll be amazed at how much more time, not to mention energy, you have in a week if you eliminate your one-sided relationships.

How to Categorize Your Relationships by Time

In order to effectively manage your relationships, you have to dedicate time to them.

Family Relationships

You need to dedicate as much time as necessary to important family relationships, with one caveat. Unless it is an emergency or special occasion, the times need to be outside your normal productive hours. That means after work, during lunch time, and so on. E-mailing, phoning, or otherwise interacting with family during the day kills your productivity and the speed of your success.

Mutually Beneficial and Supportive Relationships

Because the power of these relationships helps you meet your transformation and success goals, you should invest at least one hour per week in furthering them. That hour may be invested one-on-one or one-on-many, but it must be invested.

Because these relationships are mutually beneficial by design, it is often valuable to make multiple connections throughout the week via e-mail, phone, or in person where appropriate. I'm not suggesting that you become a nuisance or call with no reason. Be sure you have an agenda for your contact, fulfill it, and move on. Make sure you are adding something of value to the relationship so it remains mutually beneficial.

Long-Term Friends

There is no hard and fast rule about how often to see long-term friends, but ideally it would be regularly or, at the longest, every other month. Apply the same rules to family relationships as your rule of thumb.

Long-term-friend relationships have a time ebb and flow based on events that are happening around each person. Stay involved, look for meaningful ways to connect, and then refocus your effort on your profitable, productive activities. Use your interaction with your friends as a mental vacation before you return to your Fearsome Focus.

One-Sided Relationships

Spend as little time as possible here. Enough said?

Over the next hour I want you to clearly define your relationships, categorize them, and begin segmenting them. The purpose of segmenting is so you can begin spending the appropriate amount of time and effort in each relationship and then move on. Being methodical and consistent in relationships will seem a little mechanical at first, but you'll find as time goes on you are much more efficient and effective in all your relationships. At the end of the day, the process insures that everyone's needs are met, especially yours.

One-Hour Action Plan

What Specifically Do I Want to Accomplish?

Categorize my relationships.

What Specifically Am I Going to Do to Segment and Improve My Current Connections?

- Break relationships into the four defined categories: Family Relationships, Mutually Beneficial and Supportive Relationships, Long-Term Friends, One-Sided Relationships.
- Evaluate the information collected from the previous questions and work through the answers to fully understand why you're undertaking this action and what you must do to be successful.
- List the specific steps that are necessary to achieve the desired result.
- Add deadlines to each step.
- Note who will be involved in or responsible for each step if others are to be involved.
- Allocate and schedule the time for this action plan and associated steps to be implemented.
- How will you define success so we know that you've been successful?
- What is the one action step you can take this very moment that will initiate this action plan?

Personal Hour 5— Finances

9

If you look at the statistics, we worry more about finances than anything else in our lives. In my experience, the reason most people worry so much about their finances is that they don't develop a financial plan.

I have to be the first to admit I'm not crazy about finances. In fact, if I *didn't* have a plan, my bills would never get paid and I wouldn't have any kind of a financial future. So for me to be successful, I had to come up with a plan that was easy to use and nearly bullet proof. The other challenge I have is that I travel up to 200 days a year, and that makes staying on top of my finances very challenging. Since my wife owns a vibrant business with two locations, and we have a daughter, my wife doesn't have time to do everything either. A system and a plan make our financial life easy and worry free.

Prior to Setting up Any Plan

Before you set up any plan, one of the most important things you can do is spend a little time with your accountant and a financial planner.

Let me say this very plainly: If you are not an accountant and you are over 21 years old, you need an accountant. The sooner you develop a cost savings tax plan the better off you'll be. You need to pay the IRS what you are required to pay but not one cent more. Here are a few of the things you want to be sure to discuss with your accountant and financial planner.

Accountant

What experience does the accountant have in working with people in your situation to reduce taxes? There is a significant difference between being able to do your taxes accurately and helping you save on taxes. Not all accountants are adept at saving on taxes. You must find one who is willing to work with you to find creative (and legal) ways to reduce your tax burden.

You also want to find an accountant who has a style similar to your risk tolerance. If you are highly risk adverse, you'll most likely want a very conservative accountant. On the other hand, if your willingness to accept risk is high, then an accountant who will utilize the gray areas may make more sense. Ultimately, references are nearly always the best way to find good accountants. Talk to people you know and trust for the best recommendation in your area.

In addition to an accountant, you should also strongly consider speaking with a financial planner who can help you get your long-term financial life in order. If you own a business, there are many considerations you need to plan for. Whether you are a business owner or employee, you need to have plans for funding after retirement. Investing for the future is absolutely necessary, and investing regularly is mandatory. At the end of this chapter I'll share an investing ideology from James Berman, CEO of an investment advisory firm for high net worth individuals.

Setting up Your Plan

I've worked with hundreds of individuals and entrepreneurs over the past 10 years, and the ones who were most successful were those who were systematic about their financial position. They were proactive in deciding what would happen to their money and when. They were disciplined about how their money was spent, saved, or invested.

Nearly all people who are successful at managing their finances monitor them on a weekly basis. Those who are not disciplined and don't have a plan for managing their money may also monitor their finances weekly, but for an entirely different reason. Those who aren't proactive and disciplined monitor their finances to be sure they have enough to keep going!

The first step to setting up a financial plan is knowing exactly where your money is going. When I speak to people who are having financial trouble, this is the first question I ask: "Where's the money going?" Nearly every one of them believes he knows. Many feel like they can keep track of all the checks and bills in their head, but they are typically incorrect. Suze Orman, author of *The 9 Steps to Financial Freedom* (Crown Publishers, 1997), says that most people underestimate what they really need to live per month by $1,400.00.

If you've already made a financial plan, you are way ahead of the game. If you haven't, then you need to invest the time right now. Pull out your most recent bank statement and go through it. Categorize every dollar you spend. To make it easy, break it down into these categories:

1. *Housing costs*—This includes rent or mortgage, electric, gas, sewer, water, taxes, and any other essential services for maintaining your home.
2. *Medical costs*—List any required costs for maintaining your body or the bodies of your family.

3. *Transportation costs*—List any required costs for regularly scheduled transportation.

4. *Savings and investments*—List your current contribution to savings and investments.

5. *Controllable costs*—This includes all your other monthly costs, including the portion of credit card bills that doesn't cover one of the above costs, groceries, eating out, entertainment, furniture, lawn care, clothing; all your other expenses in the past month go here.

To some of you this list will seem too simplistic but it is not. The first three areas are fairly fixed in their requirements, and number four should be too (for most people it isn't). But number five is the area where you can take control of your finances and where your transformational hour will be best spent.

Once you've done this, you'll use the findings as your measuring stick for comparison during the coming months.

Focus on developing a plan that allows you to cover all of your basic financial bases. I'm intentionally keeping this simple because most people don't take any proactive role in actually planning their financial future until long after they should. If you'll invest an hour in your financial future, you'll have a great future ahead of you.

Make it Automatic

Set up as many of your bills and investments on auto pay right now. Money that you never see is money that you don't spend frivolously. Pay yourself by having money automatically sent to investment accounts and saving. By having your bills automatically paid, either through your bank or the provider, you save not only time but also fees and possibly your credit score by never being late or missing a payment.

Manage the Professionals instead of the Money

If you are not particularly crazy about managing money, then work closely with an accountant and financial planner and let them do the lion's share of the work. Spend your time managing them and analyzing their results.

Make it Digital

Use a software program like Quicken or Microsoft Money to manage your finances. By using a software program you can quickly and easily see where you stand financially at any given time. It also allows you to project where you are in relation to your goals and where potential savings or opportunities lie.

Be Frugal When You Can but Don't Step over Dollars to Pick up Dimes

Shop for bargains, use online price shopper services, and negotiate. Just be wary of how much time you are investing and what the potential payoff is. If you earn $50 an hour and it is going to take two uncompensated hours to save $25, then don't do it. If you want to spend more of your free time bargain hunting because you enjoy it, that is a bonus. Otherwise, earning time should be spent earning or multiplying your earned income beyond its current value.

Review it Regularly

Time spent in review of your finances is time well spent. Consider the time you are investing as money that you'll have at the end of the year because you studied carefully, made good decisions, and measured your success.

While researching this book, I spoke with James Berman, faculty member in the Finance and Taxation Department of the NYU School of Continuing and Professional Studies, where he teaches both corporate finance and investment. Mr. Berman believes a person should determine whether he is a gambler or an investor, and learn how to invest if he intends to do it on his own.

Investment Basics You Should Know, According to James Berman

James Berman says that, in investing, people must master their own psychology.

> Most of us have a gambling instinct when it comes to investment. The most successful investors have been able to strip out that instinct. In an hour, they should focus on how to stop looking at the stocks as gambling chips and start looking at them like real companies.

> The majority of investors are not focused on looking at their stocks as real companies. We treat them as gambling chips and we revel in it because it is exciting and easy. When managing your personal finances that approach is tantamount to disaster. When you ask people if they gamble with their savings and investments they say no, but if you look deeper, you'll find that many of them really do. The only way to change is to create a shift in their cognitive focus.

Ask Yourself This Question to Find out if You Are Gambling

Do I spend more time watching the stock price of an investment that I own than I spend reading analyst reports and annual reports? If you answer yes, you are gambling. Sitting and looking at a screen is seductive, but good investment practice is much harder; you must focus on the fundamentals of the company. Anyone can learn the skills necessary to read the reports and make good decisions. A prerequisite to reading the reports is to focus your attention in the right place.

Here is an analogy you can use to think about this question. Tennis players shouldn't look at the score. Thinking about the score is only a distraction from the essential skill of any player, which is to watch the ball. Champion investors watch the ball. Are you watching the ball or the score?

If you are behaving like a gambler you need to take active steps to shift into the other direction. According to Berman:

1. Until you shift your focus you should move your money out of individual stocks into savings or mutual funds.
2. Take a small amount of your investment capital, 1 percent or less, and invest it in a stock that you have thoroughly researched. A strong suggestion is to purchase stock of a company you are familiar with. Research the fundamentals before you make the investment. Look at annual reports and all other information.
3. Once you own the stock, turn off the ticker, trading screen, and TV and spend one hour a week surveying its fundamentals. Read every corporate filing and analyst report, listen to every earnings conference call, and read everything written in the general media and trade industry looking for trends that are favorable to that company. Look to see if the company has a real competitive advantage. Does the company participate in a growing and expanding marketplace that is likely to continue growing every year?

Simply turning off the trading screen and television will start moving you away from the gambler mentality.

If you have to watch, train yourself not to react to the screen; react instead to the information you've gained. As an investor rather than a gambler, you will keep your eye on the company, looking at changes in trends that will tell you whether to buy, sell, or hold the stock. You can ask yourself if the company's strategy makes sense.

The average investor can get as much information as the professional about the strategy, and then he has to make an educated decision about whether or not the strategy will work. Ask yourself, if this is a business you want to be in, is it succeeding or failing?

How to Determine if You Are Qualified to Invest Your Own Money

- Decide whether you are a gambler or not. If you can't change from being a gambler, you should take all the money and put it into the hands of an investment professional.
- Ask yourself honestly, do I have the knowledge to invest? Every investor needs to acquire basic knowledge. Read the classics from Benjamin Graham or any of the books about Warren Buffett and try to learn what makes a good company.

If You Decide to Invest for Yourself

Learn these basics about evaluating companies:

Only invest in companies that are strong financially. If you don't know how to recognize a strong balance sheet and cash flow, buy and read *The Interpretation of Financial Statements*, by Benjamin Graham. Once you have learned financial statement basics, you can look for companies that are strong and invest only in them.

Look for companies that have a competitive advantage, something that allows them to compete effectively with their peers. Good books to read are any of those about Warren Buffett, a book published by Morningstar called *Five Rules for Successful Stock Investing*, and *The Intelligent Investor*, by Benjamin Graham.

You'll get a lot of good ideas for investing by just looking around. Start by looking in your cupboard; it is filled with essentials made by public companies that we'll always need.

You will often do better with your own investments if you have basic skills, because many investment professionals are gamblers at heart.

Stay away from exotic strategies; they are mostly just products that Wall Street is trying to sell.

What Can You Realistically Expect if You Follow This Process?

You can expect a real change in the way you think about investment.

You will know you've been successful when you find your mind drifting toward fundamental questions such as "Will Dasini work for Coke and can it compete with Pepsi's Aquafina?" rather than looking at what is happening to a stock price in the short term.

Successful investment is about not losing money. Mark Twain said: "The thing I am concerned with is the return *of* my money, not the return *on* my money."

People should think about whether or not they'll get their money back rather than if their return will make them more successful.

Managing your finances well will serve you well for years to come, particularly in those years when you are no longer working. The hour you invest today will pay off in later hours when you can live worry free and job free.

One-Hour Action Plan

What Specifically Do I Want to Accomplish?

Develop a financial management plan.

What Specifically Am I Going to Do to Take Control of My Finances?

- Identify what your real monthly expenditures are.
- Identify all expenses that you can control and take action on those that need to be reined in.
- Set up auto pay and auto invest.
- Evaluate the information collected from the previous questions and work through the answers to fully understand why you're undertaking this action and what you must do to be successful.
- List the specific steps that are necessary to achieve the desired result.
- Add deadlines to each step.
- Note who will be involved in or responsible for each step if others are to be involved.
- Allocate and schedule the time for this action plan and associated steps to be implemented.
- How will you define success so you know you've been successful?
- What is the one action step you can take this moment that will initiate this action plan?

Personal Hour 6—
Self-Improvement

Self-improvement tends to be one of those very important things we regularly put off because, well, it is so easy to do. The problem with not constantly improving yourself is that if you are not moving forward, someone is inching past you and you are falling behind.

I'm not suggesting that self-improvement is all about competition—that is really the smallest part of it. Self-improvement is about constantly moving your evolution forward so that you never stop learning and never stop setting new goals.

When I talk about self-improvement, it can take on any form; it may be as simple as learning a new job skill that will allow you to perform at a higher level, or something as complex as going back to school to become a doctor if that is your dream.

Four Reasons Self-Improvement Efforts Typically Fail

The first reason that self-improvement efforts fail is in two parts. The first part is that it is easier to put off our own needs than to make them real.

The second part is that nearly everyone is moving through the day with maximum effort and a packed calendar; committing time for one more thing is very difficult.

The second reason most efforts fail is that we are often reluctant to invest in our improvement rather than our instant gratification. Most of us would rather buy a new boat, a new car, a new barbeque grill, or any other gadget than to actually spend our money on improving ourselves. Somewhere along the way we started believing that the company we work for should pay for our training and education. Unfortunately, that is a faulty belief. Companies to whom you have no loyalty have no compelling reason to invest heavily in you so that you can go to another company and use the newly gained training to help them profit.

The third reason that self-improvement efforts fail is that we give in to peer pressure. Our buddies laugh because we are committing the next 104 Thursdays to finally getting an MBA. Worse, they are appalled that we'd invest $3,000 in a three-day seminar that will give us access to the world's top experts and an opportunity to be trained by them. A tough question you need to ask yourself is this: If peer pressure and other people's skepticism and criticism keep you from improving your personal and professional skills, what else are they keeping you from?

The fourth reason we hesitate to improve ourselves is our past experience with transforming information into action. Experience tells us that we've invested in ourselves in the past and then not done anything with what we learned in order to give us some return on the investment. Turning information into action requires only one thing: implementation.

Implementation of new information is hard because it requires that we do something new or different. Often what we are required to do is foreign to us or will be judged by those around us. If your fear of being judged is keeping you from implementing ideas that may change your life, what else is that fear holding you back from? Nearly everyone who achieves anything significant risks being judged by someone else, twice. The first time is at the beginning, when they scoff at your effort; the next time is when they see your success and judge you in comparison to their own lack of action. Don't worry about judgment—worry about implementing the new skills and information you've obtained.

Determining the Areas of Your Life to Focus on First

If you look through the contents page in this book, you'll find a starting point for areas in your life where self-improvement is needed. But, chances are very high that you know what you need to do right now; you know which areas of your life need to be improved. Let's look a little deeper, though. Ask yourself the following questions and write down your answers.

- Which area of my life am I currently not improving that would have the most significant impact on the rest of my life if improved?
- What is the most important skill I could learn right now and why is it so important?
- When I look at the skill sets of my mentors and peers, which could I develop that would have the most significant impact on my life?
- What specifically would that impact on my life be and what would it do for me?
- What have I always wanted to study or learn but have constantly put on the back burner?
- What is the most important skill I could learn or improve right now that would expand my income, career, business, relationships?

It doesn't matter what you need or want to improve, but it is most important that you develop an attitude and habit of constantly improving yourself.

I've developed this habit over the past 20 years: I read virtually every day. I try to learn at least one new skill (notice I said learn, not perfect) each month. Then, once a year at minimum, I try to do something that requires the use of as many of my new skills as possible.

I'm a lot like you in that I don't have unlimited time to invest in self-improvement, so I look for ways to get the most intensive instruction in the shortest period of time. Let me give you an example.

I'm an avid golfer, not a good golfer by any means, but an avid golfer. In fact, if you ever want to feel better about your game, play a round with me and you'll feel like Tiger Woods.

But, since I often play golf with others in the course of business events, it was important to me to improve my skill. I decided that I wanted to go from shooting in the 115 range to being consistently below 100, and ultimately I'd like my game to be in the consistent 80s. If you are not a golfer, these scores may not mean anything to you, so let me say this: the higher the number, the worse the score. Professional golfers shoot scores in the low 60s. Most good golfers start playing when they are teenagers or younger; I started learning the game in earnest in my late 30s.

In order to improve, I recently decided to find a coach. Finding the right coach was not hard; in fact, he lived right next door. Tom Brill, a brilliant executive golf coach, was the assistant golf coach at Arizona State University in 1990–1991, Phil Mickelson's junior year.

I sat down with Tom and told him that I had one hour and wanted to improve my game. Tom asked me a few questions and gave me the following information, which allowed me to go from shooting 115s to breaking 100 the very next time I played.

What did I do with the training Coach Brill gave me? I started applying it immediately. I scheduled some time in my calendar to go to the nearest driving range twice a week during lunch break and hit a bucket of balls. I also made a list of things I wanted to remember the next time I went golfing with friends, who wouldn't mind if, during the game, I

COACH TOM BRILL'S ADVICE FOR IMPROVING YOUR GOLF GAME IN ONE HOUR

Practice your short game from 125 yards in. Seventy-five percent of your strokes are from that range.

Short game takes intelligence and imagination. If you are just a weekend golfer, you've got to pick the brains of golf professionals and golfers better than you. Learn what they do to be successful in the short game.

The short game is like pitching a baseball: You have different grips, different motions, and you want to work on ball control.

Take a lesson or two. It depends on how good you want to be. Pick a professional that you are comfortable with and take a lesson every other month. Tiger Woods is the best golfer in the world and he sees his teacher more often than that.

Phil Mickelson, best short game in golf, goes to see Dave Pells. He's the pro to the pros. You can't do it by yourself; even the greats get help.

If you go hit balls, work on effortless power instead of powerless effect; Go for a nice even steady smooth swing, so that you are making contact, hitting the shots flush in the center of the club face. The average golfer might hit two out of ten; focus on getting up to six out of ten.

Be very target oriented. Don't hit the ball just to see how far it will go. Hit it to see how accurate you can be. I was talking to Mickelson when he was in college and told him to hit the stop sign, and he asked me, "Which letter?" That's focus. Be target oriented. Make it a game. You have to hit six out of ten before you go on to the next club.

Books and videos are a great use of your time because they expand your intelligence and imagination. They are sharing their secrets with you. Even if it is just the monthly *Golf Digest*, read it, and then apply one thing.

Some of the things you see advertised on television can be good if you are a bad golfer. They will let you feel the right body mechanics for the swing, and they help you keep the swing connected.

(Continued)

COACH TOM BRILL'S ADVICE FOR IMPROVING YOUR GOLF GAME IN ONE HOUR *(Continued)*

To get your game from 100 to 80, take a lesson a month on all aspects of the game: putting, short game, long game, mental game. Do those four things every three months. You probably need to invest two hours a week working hard at it, with focused practice time. Then you need to play at least once a week.

When you are sitting at your desk, practice visualizing the game. What I'll do before I play is visualize the first four or five holes and have a game plan for how I'll play those holes. I want to get a good start and enjoy the round. I'll focus on a couple of swing thoughts for the day. My last 10 balls on the range warming up before I play will be exactly what I intend to play on the golf course. I'll hit a driver, a 7-iron, a wedge, and so forth.

Play the first four or five holes on the driving range. There are a lot of guys that want to rush into the round; go and play the first three holes on the range first. Guys who are pushing too fast, top the ball when they swing, and have no idea where it is going. They set themselves up for disaster. If you've never played the course before, then play your home course; it will get you in a good tempo.

practiced a few things I'd learned. I set a goal to put this new skill set into play when it really mattered, and I agreed to play in a golf tournament (something I'd rarely done before) in Nevada in March 2006. By committing to an event with a deadline, I'd stay focused no matter what. My goal for that tournament is not to win it—I know that won't happen—but to have my personal best score ever at that event.

Should you invest only one hour in learning a new skill or improving one? The answer is unequivocally no. It takes about 1,000 hours of practice to build expert proficiency at a new skill. I'll continue to invest hourly time at the driving range, and at least once a month I'll get additional coaching. For me golf is a business skill as much as a life skill, and it's one that I need to master.

Your ability to manage your life and time dictates how many new skills you'll want to develop at any given point in your life but, in my experience, it is a bad idea to take on more than one or two at a time if they will require significant concentrated focus to master.

Ideas for Self-Improvement That You May Want to Develop

- *A new language*—Recent studies suggest that learning a new language later in life may in fact help prevent Alzheimer's disease.
- *A hobby*—Writing, painting, flower arranging, martial arts, golf, scuba diving, travel, mountain climbing, racing, fishing, hunting, boating, dirt biking—any hobby that sounds interesting or exciting.
- *New education*—Physics, world religions, business, medicine, making money on the internet, meditation, massage therapy, or philosophy.
- *Relationship skills*—Communication, romance, dance, conflict resolution, how to flirt, how to pick up men or women.
- *Career skills*—Negotiation, sales, speaking, business writing, management, interviewing.

How to Create Continuous Self-Improvement

The important thing to remember in terms of self-improvement is striving to continuously improve. Remember, it takes about 1,000 hours of practice to develop expert proficiency at anything. If you simply pick one thing that you want to improve and develop expertise in, you can be busy for the next 19 years if you just invest an hour a week, or the next 2.73 years if you invest an hour a day. The choice of how fast is up to you, but the doing is not optional.

FITNESS COACH WENDY LUISO'S TIPS FOR IMPROVING YOUR FITNESS IN AN HOUR A WEEK

Wendy Luiso is a competitive bodybuilder and fitness trainer who focuses on helping people build a plan that can work for them. Her in-depth review of personal situations and needs allows her to customize a program for any client. When I asked her how to stay fit in an hour a week, she shared a number of ideas that anyone can use. These are her suggestions:

The first thing to do is schedule an appointment with your physician to talk about your health concerns. Find out if you have any limitations and then go to a reputable trainer. If you can focus for only one hour a week, I'd focus on cardiovascular and core training. In terms of cardiovascular, you should walk, run, stair step. Be sure that you mix it up so that your body doesn't get comfortable; keep your body guessing.

If you can focus for only an hour a week, focus over multiple days so that it isn't such a roller coaster. You want to avoid one hour of intensity and then nothing for a week. Plus, it keeps your body active.

In terms of core training, focus on your abs and lower back. Crunches are best for abs and you can do them almost anywhere.

To maintain a healthy diet and reduce your dependence on fast food, cook in advance. Focus on low-fat foods like grilled chicken and vegetables. Any meat can be easily cooked in advance (with the exception of fish). Cook yams or potatoes in advance and heat them in the microwave. Go for simplicity and variety. When at a restaurant ask for a half-order, or simply separate half the food on your plate and ask the server to bring another plate and take it away.

Don't take on too much at once. Make small changes and build them into your routine and continuously add on. Most people fail because they make exercise and diet an all-or-nothing proposition. Focus on making changes you can live with, and as you progress you'll be pleasantly surprised with what you can live with and what you can live without!

One-Hour Action Plan

What Specifically Do I Want to Accomplish?

Improve a specific area of my life.

What Area Specifically Am I Going to Improve and What Skills Do I Need to Learn?

- Clearly and specifically define what skills I need to learn in order to improve.
- List the specific steps that are necessary to achieve the desired result.
- Add deadlines to each step.
- Note who will be involved in or responsible for each step if others are to be involved.
- Allocate and schedule time for this action plan and associated steps to be implemented.
- How will you define success so we know that you've been successful?
- What is the one action step you can take this very moment that will initiate this action plan?

The reason self-improvement is so important is that it fully demonstrates what can be accomplished in a single-hour block. It also keeps you focused on things that are most important to you rather than just things you need to do. Self-improvement adds depth to your life.

Personal Hour 7— Mental Vacation

Fearsome Focus or even moderate focus can be maintained for only a limited amount of time. The same is true of real introspection and goal achievement; you must take regular mental vacations in order to achieve clarity and to give your mind a chance to drift.

There is a significant difference between taking a mental vacation and daydreaming. Mental vacations, like everything else we talk about in this book, are directed activities with a predetermined outcome.

In the case of a mental vacation, the desired outcome is to create a space in your mind designed for utter and complete relaxation. The goal is to go to that mental place and recuperate. The purpose is to give your conscious mind a rest so your unconscious mind has room to explore other opportunities.

Some of you will assume I'm talking about meditation, visualization, or some other form of relaxation, and that is part of it. But more than just meditating, the idea is to simply focus your mind away from all of your current tasks onto something you enjoy. Find a place where you can focus on something that is relaxing and unrelated to what you've been focused on.

I spend a good deal of my time focused on developing ideas for growing my clients' businesses. I am highly focused most of the time as I am looking for unique ideas or opportunities. But, about once a week, I take an hour off and simply allow my mind to expand. I either figuratively take a mental vacation or physically take one. Some days I'll simply allow my mind to drift back over the many scuba-diving trips I've taken. I'll make them as real as possible as I recall what the area looked like, what kind of sea life was present, how the water felt, what the weather was like, and what people's voices sounded like. As I do that, I focus on creating more and more detail or remembering more and more trips. I allow my mind to make all of the connections associated with those memories and I begin to relax. I mentally transport myself to a place far away from wherever and whatever I'm focused on.

If I want to take a literal mental break, I'll go and expand my mind in some way that I haven't before. I'll go someplace and study something. For example, I might go to an art museum and look at John Pitre paintings in great detail. Other times I might go to the local bookstore and pick up five books on a topic I have never studied in any detail. I allow myself to get interested and engrossed. My intention is to focus only on the activity at hand.

The subconscious part of my mental activity continues; it makes connections and conclusions based on what I've been most focused on over the past hours or days. New information or ideas often come to me during these mental vacations. You've probably had the experience of a breakthrough idea appearing to you in the shower or while you were sleeping. Your mind needs time to let all the information process in the background while you let go of the stress around finding the correct answer to your problem.

Mental vacations are not an excuse for procrastination. Mental vacations are scheduled times where you'll intentionally divert your mind from those tasks of the day or week for the purpose of gaining clarity or insight. They are there for you to find your "aha" moment.

How to Make Your Mental Vacations Powerful

The problem with relaxing and taking a mental vacation is that most people don't know how to do it. If you currently have a process that allows you to take such a vacation, it can be either in your head or outside. If playing an instrument allows you to put away all your work thoughts and relax your mind, do it. If the escape route is building bird houses, that's fine too. You will find many good activities that work for you. Tai chi, formal meditation, a trip to an art gallery or book store, driving golf balls, or staring into your fish tank are all effective ways to take a mental vacation from your Fearsome Focus.

The important key to this hour is to allow your mind to have a complete break. Remember, Fearsome Focus is tunnel vision; it is laserlike focus on an objective; there is no room for anything else. Mental vacations allow room for whatever is needed for your mind to function at the highest level.

You can take mental vacations once a day, 12 minutes at a time, or you can take them once a week, an hour at a time, whatever you find most effective.

Here is a place for you to start. Rather than gathering around the coffee machine at break time, close your door, go to your car, or hide in the conference room. Get in a comfortable position and relax. Begin to imagine your perfect day, your perfect vacation, or your perfect retirement. Make it real by taking time to focus on the sounds and images in your mind. Add a little more depth and complexity by mentally exploring how you'd feel in that situation. Notice the scents in this lovely place. Then, continue to add layer upon layer of detail until you are fully entranced by your creation. Set a timer if necessary, just in case you drift off or forget to get back to reality. During this time, focus on breathing deeply in through your nose, deep into your stomach, down into your hips and out again through your mouth.

If you find your thoughts drifting back to the issue you've been focused on, simply acknowledge the thought, allow it to pass, and then continue to build your utopia. When you first start taking these mental vacations, you may not notice anything at all other than your being more relaxed and refreshed when you go back to work. But, as you progress, be ready for ideas that run through your head spontaneously about *any* project or idea you've been working on. The idea is not to take a mental vacation with the purpose of finding an idea; it is to give your mind a rest but to be present enough to capture an idea if it appears.

If you decide to do a physical activity like going to the park, arranging flowers, or doing yoga, the same process applies. Do that activity up to the point where it is all you are focusing on, but be present for the ideas that present themselves.

There is probably no great mind in the world, living or dead, who does/did not take regular mental breaks in order to recharge the brain. Think of it this way: If you were exercising and working at maximum exertion, at some point your muscles would fatigue; you couldn't do another step. Your brain is no different when focused on completing a task; it must have time to relax and recover.

Here is one last thought on how to spend your mental vacation. Massage is a powerful tool for mental vacations because it does two things at once: It allows you time to physically relax because of the effect of the massage, plus is gives you time for mental relaxation. In many cases you'll go into a trance-like state because you are so relaxed. You'll know you are there because you are not quite asleep but not quite awake; you are just deeply relaxed. I keep a small voice recorder handy when I get a massage just so I can note the ideas that come while I'm in the relaxed state.

Give mental vacations a try. If you'll follow the program of doing them in earnest once a day or once a week, you'll be amazed at the progress you'll make in a single hour.

One-Hour Action Plan

What Specifically Do I Want to Accomplish?

Take a mental vacation.

What Specifically Am I Going to Do to Segment and Improve My Current Connections?

- Define an activity that allows the mind to completely relax and move away from pressing thoughts, focus, or effort.
- List the specific times you'll take a mental vacation.
- Mark the times in your calendar.
- How will success be defined so you know you've been successful?
- What is the one action step you can take this very moment that will initiate this action plan?

Personal Hour 8— Envisioneering: Creating a Master Life Vision

Vision without action is a daydream. Action without vision is a nightmare.

—Japanese proverb

At some time in our lives we get to a point where we are unsure about what to do next, what our purpose is, what we want out of life.

Far too often we choose either to do nothing, or simply accept what life hands us and justify it as being part of the experience we had to go through or as a lesson we had to learn. But the reality of life is that you get exactly what you ask for.

You must have a vision for your life, something more compelling than your everyday distractions, if you are to reach your potential, accomplish something significant, or, more important, achieve the level of happiness and personal satisfaction you deserve. Envisioneering™ is an effective process for clearly defining and mapping your master life vision.

What is a vision and how do you create one?

Many of us have thought of it as something that companies do, a statement they create to guide them, which is typically ambiguous and could apply to anyone. A real vision is something much more powerful.

Hitler had a vision. It was awful, but so compelling that he was able to sway masses of people. Martin Luther King had a vision, one so powerful and compelling that he was willing to give his life for it, and ultimately he did. In the meantime, he changed the United States forever. Albert Einstein had a vision that drove him and he ultimately changed reality and physics forever.

Merriam-Webster's Collegiate Dictionary defines vision as: **1 a :** something seen in a dream, trance, or ecstasy; *especially* : a supernatural appearance that conveys a revelation; **b :** an object of imagination; **c :** a manifestation to the senses of something immaterial. **2 a :** the act or power of imagination; **b (1) :** mode of seeing or conceiving (2) : unusual discernment or foresight <a man of vision>; **c :** direct mystical awareness of the supernatural usually in visible form.

The commonality found in Hitler, King, and Einstein was their ability to manifest a vision and dedicate their unwavering focus and belief to achieve it. They imagined something so clearly that they manifested it (definition: *to make evident or certain by showing or displaying*) not just to their senses, but to the senses of those around them. When Einstein imagined himself riding a beam of light into space, he had a revelation. Once these men had the vision and were focused, they unleashed the power of manifestation. The power of manifestation says whatever you can conceive you can create, and the unseen forces of the mind, the universe, and the human spirit will attach themselves to your undertaking and drive you successfully through your vision until it becomes reality.

The power of manifestation has been the subject of hundreds of books, lectures, and studies, and all of them agree that you can manifest the life you want if only you will chose to do so. Many of those books provide ideas of things you can manifest, and a few even give you some idea of the roadmap to follow, but those maps are only correct for the person who wrote them, not necessarily for the person reading the book.

The only plan that is perfect for you and will insure your success is your Master Life Vision: a living, breathing matrix that embodies and represents the "you" that you design. It is not static, but rather fully evolutionary in its exterior and yet substantial in its core. If you look at a city, the basis of the city remains intact even as the city evolves into a much larger organism.

Nearly all of the studies mentioned above have missed the real secret.

Hidden Secret of Manifestation Revealed

First say to yourself what you would be; and then do what you have to do.

—Epictetus (55-135 AD) Roman Philosopher

The secret of manifesting anything you desire in life or business has four requirements that must be fulfilled in order to fully unleash the power of manifestation.

The first requirement of the secret: you must specifically define what you want. You get what you ask for in exactly the format you ask for it. If you ask for something that is one dimensional, lacking in depth or description, that is what you'll get and it will not fulfill you. On the other hand, if you ask for something in rich detail, imbued with emotion and feeling, layered with experiences, and something that you can see so clearly in your mind that it becomes tangible, then you'll get that too and it will be rich and empowering.

The second requirement is understanding how what you want fits into your master vision of life. Remember, your mind can work in only one direction at a time. If you only focus on getting a new car, you cannot focus on getting the life you really want. So the second part of the equation is placing what you want in the proper perspective of your Master Life Vision. Where does what you want fit and what does it really do for you? If you can answer those questions, manifestation is already beginning to happen.

The third requirement of the secret is giving your Master Life Vision power. Hold it powerfully in your mind and create it in the physical realm. One of the most effective methods to create your vision in the physical realm is to write it down on paper or in your word processor. A word processor is particularly powerful because, when the plan evolves, it is easy to add and edit the next layer of texture and experience. A corollary to this part of the secret is that you are in control. You can alter your vision whenever it is appropriate.

The final part of the equation is to activate your Master Life Vision. To show a commitment to the life you desire to create, you must take action toward attainment as soon as you are through creating your Master Life Vision. By doing so, you activate the plan; your vision comes alive in front of your eyes and it becomes a powerful, vital force pulling you toward your fullest potential. Additionally, you are able to more effectively pull in the resources and people needed to fulfill your vision.

> *Vision without action is merely a dream. Action without vision just passes the time. Vision with action can change the world.*
> —Joel A. Barker, American businessman, consultant, and author

The more compelling your vision, the easier it will be to take the first steps. So add layer upon layer of thought and ideas; create the most brilliant picture of reality you can imagine. Go back to it like an artist and add another color, element, stroke, or feature to make it spring to life.

Power Questions to Jumpstart Your Master Life Vision

There is only one success—to spend your life in your own way.
—Christopher Morley

The following questions are a starting point for you to use in creating your Master Life Vision. These questions will give you an idea of how to achieve the depth and dimension necessary for creating a compelling vision unique to you. They will help you develop the structure needed to completely build the matrix of your life.

These questions are most effective if you write down every answer that comes to mind. Do this with each question. If you think of another question that would better define your vision, write that question down and include your answers. Answer the questions in the first person: "I am" or "I do."

Be sure to answer these questions as if you are already living your perfect life. If you are not sure how to answer the question, write down the first thing that comes to your mind, or what you think someone you deeply respect and trust might say.

Note: Some people find it useful to do this exercise twice: the first time to write down what you currently do in response to the question, and the second time to answer it as you would in your perfect life. Sometimes it's helpful to compare your current life map with the one that leads you to manifest your true being.

My Perfect Life

- What is a perfect day in my perfect life like?
- What is the first thing I do when I get out of bed?
- What will I have done the night before to make this day perfect?
- What will I listen to? Read? Research? Explore?
- What exercise will I do?

- What will I eat?
- How will I relax? What will that feel like?
- What is important to me?
- What is my health like? Why?
- How do I overcome setbacks and obstacles?
- What do I do when I feel stuck?
- How do I reward myself?
- What music do I listen to?
- What do I create?
- What am I thankful for?
- What have I done so far to get to the mental and physical state I'm in?
- Who will be there with me?
- What are they adding to my life? How specifically?
- Where will I be specifically? Country, town, environment?
- What does my house look like in detail? Inside? Outside?
- What smells will I smell?
- What will I do that day? In the morning, afternoon and evening?
- Who are my mentors and what are they mentoring me in?
- Which past and present will I still want in my life?
- How did I find my current and past mentors?
- What am I able to do better than anyone else?
- What am I an expert at?
- What knowledge do I have that others seek?
- What will I get out of living my perfect day?
- How will I feel? What will I have accomplished?
- What is the last thing I'll do before I go to bed?

My Perfect Career or Business
- What perfect career have I created for myself?
- Alternatively: What perfect business have I built for myself?
- Why?

- What do I get from my career or business? Money? Recognition? Satisfaction?
- How much of each?
- Is that enough?
- What am I giving back to my family? City? State? Country? Humanity?
- How do I feel when I experience my career daily? Fulfilled? Excited?
- How did I get to this place in my life?
- What did I learn?
- What did I experience?
- What did I create?
- How did those tie together to create this perfect situation?
- How big is my career? Am I in control?
- What do I do for the people around me who support my career or business?
- How specifically?
- When will my career or business be complete?
- How will I know specifically when I've achieved all I should?
- How did I create my perfect career or business?
- What did I do specifically?
- Who helped me? (This can be an actual person you already know or a description of the people by characteristics that helped you along the way.)
- How did I meet those people?
- What did they get out of helping me?
- What am I known for?
- What do my family and/or loved ones get from my career or business?
- What limitations, obstacles, or roadblocks did I overcome to get here?
- How did I overcome?
- How does my career or business fit into and support my perfect life?

My Perfect Relationship

- Who is the person in my life that completes me?
- What qualities about that person make them perfect for me?
- What do they look like specifically? What color is their hair? Their eyes? What is their build?
- What do they love most about me?
- How are they brilliant?
- How do they complete me specifically? What do they add to the equation I don't already have?
- What kind of person are they?
- What do they do for a living?
- How educated are they? Formally? Informally?
- What do they do for fun?
- What do they do for me that no one else on the planet can?
- How do they look at me that lets me know they love me even when nobody else knows what that look means?
- How does my body feel when I'm with them?
- How do my emotions feel? Which emotions am I most aware of when I'm with them?
- What do they know about me that no one else does?
- How do I show them how I love them?
- How do they react to that?
- What would I do for them that no one else in the world would do, without hesitation?
- What is our partnership like?
- What friends will we have?
- What kids do we have or do we have kids?
- What is our friendship like?
- Give me an example of how it would be?
- What is our sex life like?
- What is our time apart like?
- What are our vacations like?

- Where do we go?
- What do we do?
- What do we talk about in the privacy of our home?
- What do we do together that we are known for?
- How do we disagree?
- How are we different from one another?
- What does he or she smell like?
- What kind of a thinker is he or she?
- What kind of music do they listen to?
- What kind of movies do they like?
- What is the one dream they have that you are supporting in every way you can?
- How did I know when I found the perfect partner?
- What limiting beliefs, emotions, thoughts, or ideas did I overcome to attract the perfect partner?
- How did I overcome?
- How does my partner fit into my perfect life?

My Perfect Spirituality

- What does spirituality mean to me?
- What do I believe?
- Why?
- What am I learning?
- What am I exploring?
- What beliefs do I have that are mainstream?
- What beliefs to I have that are not mainstream?
- Am I religious?
- How will I know when I've become a spiritual person?
- What will be present in my life?
- How will I feel?
- Which books am I reading?
- How do I practice my spirituality?

- How does my spiritual life manifest itself?
- What is my God like? (Describe your God in vivid detail, what your God would know, do, be.)
- How are others impacted by my spirituality?
- What did I do along the way to get to this place of being?
- How do I know I've reached an appropriate place spiritually?
- Who are the great teachers I've studied?
- How many other people are like me?
- What limiting thoughts or beliefs did I overcome to get to this place?
- How did I overcome them?
- Where does my spirituality fit into my perfect life?

My Perfect Financial Situation
- How much money do I have?
- How much wealth do I have? (Investments, savings etc.)
- What trappings of wealth do I have? (Cars, homes, boats, yachts, planes, etc.)
- What does my wealth get for me?
- How does my wealth make me feel?
- How do I use my wealth to make the world a better place?
- What is the next big thing I'll do with my money?
- How do those around me feel about me and my wealth?
- How do I get my wealth?
- What is something surprising I am able to do with money?
- What things do I buy easily?
- How did my life change as a result of my wealth?
- What is my attitude about money? Why?
- If I need more money tomorrow, how do I get it?
- What does money get for me?
- How specifically did I learn to have the wealth that I have?
- What do I study? What do I read? How often?

- Are there people in my life who help me with my money?
- What do those people do?
- Why did I decide to have them help me?
- What obstacles or limiting behaviors about money have I overcome?
- How did I overcome?
- How does my wealth fit into my perfect life?

Miscellaneous Questions
- Who are my friends?
- How did they become my friends?
- Are they the same friends I had before I developed my perfect life?
- If not, why? If so, why?
- Whom am I friendly with who is famous? Infamous?
- How often do I spend time in solitude thinking?
- What is my contribution to the world?
- What chances am I willing to take?
- How will I know when it is time to take them?
- Why am I willing to take those chances?
- What do I look back at and wonder why I took so long to overcome it?
- Where was I stuck and what did I do to overcome it?
- How is my relationship with each member of my family and what did I do to get it to this point?
- Who did I forgive and let go that freed me? What did I do to forgive them? How did that feel? What was the most significant feeling I had from letting it go? What do I have now as a result?
- How do I keep myself in perspective?
- What do I do to continue to explore and learn?
- What does thinking mean to me?
- What is exploring to me?
- What is experiencing to me?
- What am I still curious about?

- What is a never-ending source of amazement for me?
- What hobbies do I have?
- What fulfillment do I get from my hobbies?
- How am I creative?
- What did I want more than anything else that I now have? What do I still want more than anything?
- Where have I visited? Where do I still want to visit?
- What questions do I have left to ask that I haven't yet?

Final Steps to Success

Now that you've delved deeply into your future self, you have created an outline of your Master Life Vision. You have the structure to find your life purpose and you have a roadmap specific to you and created by you.

You've already begun to manifest your perfect life! Congratulations!

Consolidation is the final step in putting the pieces of your plan together. In narrative format, write a paragraph or two detailing your perfect life. It should breathe life and power into your Master Life Vision, and give an overview of your perfect life above.

Combine in writing the essence of the experiences, ideas, thoughts, desires, dreams, deadlines, and abilities you outlined above. Keep the result with you so when you get frustrated, sidetracked, or unsure you can pull it out and remind yourself of your goals for achieving the perfect life. Your written reminder should vividly describe the life you desire and what that accomplishment means to you.

Your Master Life Vision describes you, your purpose, and your mission. If you're unsure whether you are moving closer or farther away from your perfect life, you can reflect. You also have a perfect and concise description of the life you desire; the self you are manifesting.

You'll use your Master Life Vision to track your path and acknowledge manifestation as it occurs. Each time a piece of your vision is achieved, write on your plan the date it occurred and the circumstance by which it came about. You'll be in awe of how you manifested what you imagined it to be.

As you completed this exercise you undoubtedly wrote down skills you acquired along the way, experiences you had, things you studied, and more. Take the time to write those down now below each of the following:

- Skills I will acquire to create my perfect life.
- Experiences I will have to create my perfect life.
- Places I will visit to create my perfect life.
- People I need to meet or cultivate to create my perfect life.
- Timelines and deadlines I need to be aware of to create my perfect life.
- The next three steps I need to take along the path to my perfect life.
- The first step I will take today toward my perfect life, thus unleashing the power of manifestation.

As time goes on, review the questions again; add more texture, layers, and depth as appropriate. Be happy with what you've brought to life and feel free to give yourself big challenges or to bask in the contentment of success.

Activate your vision now, take the first step, and you'll be pulled rapidly toward the life of your vision by the unseen force inside. The only thing stopping you from having everything you've ever dreamed of or desired is your willingness to take the first step.

One-Hour Action Plan

What Specifically Do I Want to Accomplish?

Create a master life vision.

What Specifically Am I Going to Do to Create My Master Life Vision?

- Work through all of the questions listed above to develop my vision.
- Create or reexamine and improve my vision.
- Evaluate the information I collected from the previous questions and work through the answers to fully understand why I'm undertaking this action and what I must do to be successful.
- List the specific steps that are necessary to achieve the desired result.
- Add deadlines to each step.
- Note who will be involved in or responsible for each step if others are to be involved.
- Allocate and schedule the time for this action plan and associated steps to be implemented.
- How will you define success so we know that you've been successful?
- What is the one action step you can take this very moment that will initiate this action plan?

Personal Hour 9—Overcome Your Fear and Reinvent Yourself

When I talk about reinventing yourself, I mean in all the possible ways you can reinvent yourself. You can reinvent your life, your career, or your business. Reinventing yourself means making a significant change in the course of your everyday actions. Reinventing yourself may happen often, or once in your life, or for many, never. Reinvention is always good because it gives you a chance to experience something that will forever change your outlook on life and business.

The Fear Factor

Fear is the most significant barrier that faces anyone who sets out to create something new. Fear is a powerful motivator because as humans we are wired for self-preservation. Yet, if we had given in to the impulse for self-preservation, we would have never conquered new lands, built structures of unparalleled grandiosity, or asked the pretty girl we just met for a date. Fear is a belief based sometimes on past experience, but often based solely on what we think will happen. Fear stifles opportunity even when we have no empirical evidence that indicates we will fail or that something bad will happen. We simply use fear to justify potential failure.

The physical sensation of fear or pain is not what keeps you from doing what matter most. It is the anticipation of imagined outcomes that prevents success. When confronted suddenly with a fearful event, you react and survive. When presented with an opportunity that contains an element of uncertainty, change, or question, you begin anticipating. Once you start to anticipate, your mind builds scenarios that create fear more quickly than you can overcome them. The mind is so powerful that it can instantly stall progress and potential.

How to Overcome Fear

Overcoming fear is quite simple; take Educated Action. Educated Action overcomes fear and reduces the likelihood of failure or realization of hypothetical disastrous outcomes. Real information and feedback give you the only reliable tool for determining what happens next. I'm not saying you can't look at scenarios and weigh them in relationship to their likelihood of success; you should use your critical thinking skills. What I am saying is that if you take no action to overcome your fear, you'll get only reinforcing feedback that encourages no action at all. Educated Action overcomes fear.

There are two ways of overcoming fear. The first is to do something with no education and accept the result of your action. Think of that method as the "poke the wild animal with the stick and see what happens" method. The second and more appropriate way is to employ Educated Action and arm yourself with a reasonable number of facts before you take any action.

When I worked on a SWAT team we didn't just let new people jump right into the fray the next time there was an emergency event; we trained them first. We gave them a new set of skills and then had them practice those skills in controlled environments. By giving them Educated Action steps, they learned to respond. Their fear went away because they got real feedback based on real life experiences. By knowing the facts about what was most likely to happen, people who were reinventing themselves as SWAT team members were able to overcome their fear and significantly increase their likelihood of success.

In the course of my life, I've reinvented myself a number of times. When I was growing up, I wanted to be a cowboy, a police officer, and a soldier, and I'd been each by the time I was 25. I'd also been a business owner and author, two things I hadn't considered, which required me to reinvent who I was. In order to be successful at each opportunity, I had to take the experience I could leverage from the previous incarnation and quickly learn new skills in order to achieve success in my new life. It also required that I take Educated Action steps in order to position myself for success.

How to Determine Your Educated Action Steps

The simplest path to Educated Action is education and emulation.

When you set out to reinvent yourself, invest some time studying what is required to be the new you. Read books and magazines, do research, watch television programming, study the leaders in any field and see what they did to get where they are today. Learn as much as you can about what is going to be required of you.

After you begin to study what is important, emulate those people who are most successful. Determine what each person does in order to be successful. Look at their skills, attitudes, beliefs, and actions. Begin to do some of the things they do. Even ask one of those people to mentor you through the process. Mentoring can save countless hours in your transformation.

Finally, put together your action plan. Your plan will be determined by the complexity of what you have to learn or do in order to complete your reinvention. Be specific about the steps needed to achieve success.

I discovered that reinventing myself got easier each time I did it, and I brought a unique set of skills and experience to bear on the next opportunity. Those unique skills and opportunities have created strong competitive advantages in my new position. The most important skill set might be that of reinvention.

Reinventing yourself requires you to make a fundamental shift in your current belief structure. It is common to define yourself by a self-prescribed label. You are a businessman, a postal worker, a grocery clerk, or a flight attendant. Whatever label you've developed tends to color your view of the world around you. Through this label you have created a set of beliefs that you use to evaluate everything.

To change, you must suspend your beliefs for a while. You have to believe that change is possible and be willing to test it. Reinvention starts at a belief level and ends at a visible change level and not vice versa. Nearly everyone who tries to reinvent themselves tries the "fake it until they make it" method, or they throw themselves into the new situation and sink or swim. Neither method is appropriate.

Faking it until you make it is some of the worst advice ever given, and I'll tell you why. First, people who are adept at your new life or skill will see right through your attempt to fake it. Second, you can never have the depth of experience or opportunity that exists if you follow a real plan for reinventing yourself.

Throwing yourself into your new life without preparation is almost as bad as faking it until you make it. While the sink or swim method can work, you often sink. The more failures you have the more likely it is you'll return to your old behavior, thus reinforcing your previous beliefs about why you can't change. The result is that you'll either have no success or your success will be hampered and slowed along the way.

How to Reinvent Yourself

The first step to reinvention is to take stock of your current skills and see which ones are applicable in your new incarnation. By leveraging your existing skill set, you set the stage for the fastest possible assimilation of a new life.

Next, assess the skills and other requirements to achieve success. What specifically will you need to learn, whom will you need to meet, and what will you need to do in order to create a whole new you? Write those things down in detail now.

Next, honestly assess your core beliefs about change, about being someone different. Ask yourself and honestly answer these very tough questions:

- Why am I recreating my life and what will it do to me, my family, and my friends? What will happen to me mentally, physically, emotionally, and spiritually if I make this change?
- What will happen to my relationships with my family, my spouse, my children, my friends, my community, and myself if I make this change?
- What am I willing to sacrifice if necessary in order to achieve this change?
- What will happen if I am unsuccessful in making this transition?
- Who will support me unconditionally through this transformation? Who will abandon me?
- At the end of the change, what will be so much better about my life and situation that making the change regardless of the sacrifice will make the change worth it?

Finally, map out your action steps. Determine exactly what skills you need to learn first and how you will acquire them. By making a precise action plan you'll quickly create the change you desire.

One-Hour Action Plan

What Specifically Do I Want to Accomplish?

Reinvent myself.

What Specifically Am I Going to Do to Reinvent Myself or an Area of My Life or Career?

- Define the area of life or career that needs to be reinvented.
- Evaluate the information collected from the previous questions and work through the answers to fully understand why you're undertaking this action and what must be done to be successful.
- List the specific steps that are necessary to achieve the desired result.
- Add deadlines to each step.
- Note who will be involved in or responsible for each step if others are to be involved.
- Allocate and schedule the time for this action plan and associated steps to be implemented.
- How will success be defined so you know when you've been successful?
- What is the one action step you can take this very moment that will initiate this action plan?

Reinventing yourself or particular areas of your life or career on a regular basis can be one of the most empowering (and profitable) experiences of your life. If you are not continually evolving then you are stagnating and ultimately dying. Your life is up to you, and how you create it will determine exactly what you get.

What part of you should you reinvent today?

CHAPTER

Business Hour 1— Finding Your Business Focus

14

Spending an hour finding your business focus will change your business forever. Even when businesses are running well you need to find your focus in order to create endless improvement.

Finding business focus means focusing on your business processes and on the business itself. Michael Gerber was one of the first people to point out that people don't work on their business, they work in their business. Few people really understand what working on your business involves: it means finding a particular area to work on so that it will systematically improve. Once that one has been improved, you move to the next area and thus continue to work your way through the business. The result is that you are able to identify areas that need your specific attention and focus your efforts to create rapid change.

I spoke with Fortune 500 business strategist Chet Holmes, who explained why CEOs and managers should commit to focusing on their business in this way. He said that, while most people don't work on their business at all, if they devote an hour a week to the business they can make incremental improvements.

With all of his clients Chet uses an exercise that helps them determine their focus. He asks the company to gather together the appropriate staff who can help move the company forward. Everyone gets immunity, but there is no airing petty grievances. The focus is to identify real opportunities for improvement. He asks everyone to name two or three things that need to change in order to make the company smarter, faster, better, more productive, and so on. He records all the answers and prioritizes them. Everyone gets three votes. Their first vote is worth three points, the second is worth two, and the third is worth one. The staff people get to vote on three things they believe should be focused on first. Once the votes are cast, the three areas of focus with the most votes are the first to get attention. Later, the staff works its way down the list. This way, the CEO doesn't have to come up with all the ideas. He simply facilitates development of the ideas and then goes to work on the necessary action to correct or implement them.

Breaking out the Operational Units

One of the most efficient ways of determining focus areas is to break the business into separate operational units. By doing this, you can focus on every area of your business. There is typically no area that cannot be improved. For most businesses, this means breaking the company into sales, marketing, operations, financial operations, manufacturing, service delivery, and human resources. You can break the areas down even further after you have segregated the business into operational units.

Sales

Spend an hour a week focusing on your sales efforts and team. If you want to understand what is happening in your marketplace, spend some time with your sales team. These are typically the first people to notice a change in the market because of their frequent customer interactions.

If you have someone managing sales, spend your sales hour mentoring the manager or helping him develop his focus on the department. Look closely at what you can do to improve ROI on sales effort investment. Work to develop strategies to shorten the sales cycle or monetize it in areas where you've traditionally not done anything. Your focus in sales should be to look closely for ways to create new opportunities for profit.

Marketing

Evaluate your marketing efforts often and critically. You'll find opportunities for savings and new customer acquisition opportunities. Most CEOs ignore marketing. But by spending an hour focused inside your marketing machine you'll find new ideas for acquiring customers and creating new product or service lines that can bolster your income.

Spending time focused on customer experience can be a profitable review. Know exactly what your customers experience in their interactions with your company. Understand where the process works and where it breaks down. Once you understand the process, you can continuously improve it. In today's market one of the single biggest competitive advantages is a compelling customer experience. Create a reason for customers to do business with you. Make customers and their experience your focus and you'll discover new ideas every day that will set you apart from any competition.

Operations

Spend some time focused on all areas that help your business run. Operations is one of the most overlooked areas for improvement. Your goal should be to improve efficiency. Anything you can do to make your organization more efficient, lean, and proactive will have far-reaching impact throughout the organization.

Financial Operations

One of the most overlooked areas in financial operations is tax strategy. Nearly all small and midsized businesses pay more tax than they need to. Spend some of your focus time reviewing your tax situation with both your accountant and a tax attorney. Many times there are simple restructuring strategies you can use to save you thousands of dollars.

You should spend time focused on evaluating the business for cost-saving opportunities. I have yet to work with an organization, one that is having problems or even ones that are not, that can't add money right back to their bottom line by smart cost-cutting initiatives. The first place to look is at old systems and relationships. Many times you'll find you are still being billed for things you no longer need or use. This is especially true when it comes to services and subscriptions.

Manufacturing or Service Delivery Units

This is an area that you probably already spend a lot of time on but usually in a problem-solving mode. Proactively looking at these units will often lead to profitable discoveries about new products, services, manufacturing opportunities, or service delivery options. Your responsibility is to look at these areas for ways to increase profitability. Evaluate processes, people, tools, and best practices to find incremental improvements.

Human Resources

It is a cliché, but it's true: the most valuable asset in your company is your people. What you don't hear is that your people can be your most costly asset if they are the wrong people.

The reason this area is so often overlooked is that it is not usually understood by management or the CEO. The process is avoided and ignored by hiring someone to handle it and then leaving him alone.

Virtually every manager who is involved in hiring staff should go through detailed interview training. People make hiring decisions based on poor reasons, most often because they don't have the necessary skills to properly evaluate an employee. It is important to move candidates through a specific process that gathers information, challenges them formally and informally, tests their knowledge and skills, and assesses personality. Without that kind of process, you stack the odds against yourself in terms of hiring star performers.

Another focus area in human resources is creating effective and functional job descriptions that clearly define the expectations of the position. When effective and functional job descriptions are combined with employee modeling—that is, identifying the most valuable skills in your top employees in every position—you create a powerful hiring solution.

Because this is such an important and potentially valuable area to evaluate, you may want to move human resources higher on your scale of one-hour investment priorities.

Power Questions for Finding Business Focus

- If I had unlimited time and resources, what is the one area I'd focus on in my business?
- What would that do for the business?

- What areas of the company need attention now?
- What areas of the company require my insight and focus to move them forward?
- When was the last time I formally polled my managers and employees for ideas for improvement?
- Which employees in my organization are highly effective and should be modeled?
- Which employees in the organization are highly inefficient?
- What was the last project I proactively identified, evaluated, and created change or improvement around that was not brought to my attention as a "fire" that I had to put out?
- Where do I want my business to be this time next year? Five years from now? Ten years from now? What am I working on that is readying the business to achieve those goals?

Open Your Eyes

Spending an hour a week for only a few weeks analyzing what is happening in your business will give you insights you likely haven't had for years.

As business owners and managers, we spend too much time focused on day-to-day activities and we fail to see everything that is really happening. Look at your business with eyes wide open. When I go into a company, I'm able to make dramatic changes because I see the company for the way it is, not the way I believe it to be or wish it were after having worked in it for years.

In order to develop that wide-open vision, spend some time questioning things, even things you think you understand. Ask people why they are doing what they are doing; have them explain the process. Another great technique is to go to another business and evaluate it for an hour. I've done this in the past with business associates. I simply have them come to my office and ask my staff questions. I have them observe my processes and my day-to-day operations. I do the same for them, and then we sit down and discuss our findings. The results have been nothing short of amazing.

Be sure, when you ask questions or look for feedback from employees, that you listen reflectively and don't judge or criticize their answers. Don't leave them with the idea that everything they tell you will happen, but don't be defensive either. It is important that your staff feels comfortable giving you honest and insightful feedback when you ask for it. Biting your tongue may be the hardest thing you do, but it will pay off.

Looking at your business with eyes wide open is an experience that, once you've done it, you'll want to repeat often.

Measure Your Improvement

Once you've started finding your business focus, it is important to focus on making consistent improvements. Focus on one area for as many weeks as needed before you move to the next. Make sure you've optimized one process before you move on to the next. Measure the starting point of your effort and keep track of your progress. One of the best ways to stay on track is to see the improvements you are making. Remember, you are no different from any other human being; we are all rewarded by achievement and likely to do more of the things we feel we are making progress on.

The Power of Finding Your Business Focus

From following this process you'll become more aware of your business and the opportunities in it. As you look closer and closer at your business, you begin to notice more detail. Then, when you pull back and look at the big picture, you'll notice how all the fine details work together and you can instantly see where bigger processes need work.

Don't forget, there is no reason you have to create all the solutions yourself. Your hour may be best spent focusing others' actions to drive the business toward a better place. Your hour is just focused on identification and solution ideation.

One-Hour Action Plan

What Specifically Do I Want to Accomplish?

Find my business focus.

What Specifically Am I Going to Do to Identify the First Area of Focus?

- Identify possible areas of focus and prioritize them by their impact on profitability and efficiency.
- Evaluate the information collected from the previous questions and work through the answers to fully understand why you're undertaking this action and what you must do to be successful.
- List the specific steps necessary to achieve the desired result.
- Add deadlines to each step.
- Note who will be involved in or responsible for each step if others are to be involved.
- Allocate and schedule the time for this action plan and associated steps to be implemented.
- How will you define success so we know you've been successful?
- What is the one action step you can take this very moment that will initiate this action plan?

Business Hour 2— Time Management

By this stage in your life you've undoubtedly read books on time management. You've probably also tried a number of different time-management tools and found some are effective and some just don't work. It is time to get in control of your time once and for all.

Here is the reality we all have to face right now. Nearly all of the time management books were written before the information explosion of the last 10 years. I heard a statistic recently that we now get more information on a daily basis than our great-grandparents got in a year at the turn of the twentieth century. With all this information interrupting us throughout the day, becoming focused, consistent, and methodical is the only way to succeed in managing time.

The Discipline of Time Management

Time management isn't as much about managing minutes as it is about being disciplined. Having the will and focus to do the same thing every day in order to be productive is one of the most empowering skills you can develop. But, like all new skills, it requires focus and determination to succeed.

I ask everyone I work with to do this exercise for one week prior to engaging in a serious time-management transformation. Keep your calendar as you normally would; schedule your appointments and your time. Then, keep a separate paper calendar where you can keep track of your time in 15-minute increments. Go about your day as usual but keep your paper calendar with you. If for any reason you are interrupted or off-task from your main calendar even for a minute, write down the time of the interruption, the amount of time invested, and what the cause of the interruption was. An interruption is defined as anything that is not scheduled on your calendar. If you take a phone call, you write down the start time and the finish time. If someone walks into your office and speaks with you, you write it down. If you are trying to do two things at once and one isn't scheduled, write it down. If you check e-mail or surf the web, write it down. Write down your interruptions as you go; the minute you get distracted or interrupted, write down the start time. As soon as you are back on task, write down the finish time.

At the end of each working day, before you go home, you go back through each event and assign it a number:

1. Urgent, interruption could not be avoided.
2. Important, needed to happen within one hour.
3. Moderate, could have been rescheduled for up to four hours later.
4. Low, could have been rescheduled for up to eight hours later or the following day.
5. Time Killer, didn't need to be done but got attention anyway.

After each number, write down one of these two designations:

I–I must do this task.

D–Delegate—This task could have been delegated.

This is an exercise in feedback and awareness and the beginning of disciplining yourself for time-management success.

Remember I said earlier that time management is not much about managing minutes, but about disciplining yourself? This is your first step in creating discipline. What happens by going through this exercise for a week is that you begin to mentally categorize interruptions. As you get an interruption you'll quickly be able to assign it a number between 1 and 5 and determine what to do.

Here is another way to look at the numbers and how to handle each one.

1. *Urgent.* Take action, do what is required as expediently as possible. Reschedule an equivalent number of less important things on your calendar so that you can still accomplish the most important tasks of the day.

2. *Important.* Complete as much of the task at hand as possible, prioritize what has to happen next, then take action on the interruption.

3. *Moderate.* Adjust your calendar to fit the interruption within four hours. At the appropriate time take focused action. Once scheduled, return to your original focus.

4. *Low.* Schedule at an appropriate time in the future and return to task.

5. *Time Killer.* Take no action, keep your focus on your task; if the interruption is something you really want to look at later, schedule it at a time when you are free.

Time Killers

No one is perfect at managing all the interruptions every day, but you can come very close. Discipline means being able and willing to do what others don't do, even if you'd prefer not to at the time.

Here is a list of the most frequent time killers that we all face each day.

- Nonessential e-mail
- Web surfing
- Water cooler conversations
- Long breaks
- Television and radio (The ads are designed to break your attention and get you to listen to them.)
- Cell phones
- Drop-in visitors
- Doing unscheduled activities just because you thought of them and they are more interesting than what you are working on
- Phone conversations with family and nonbusiness friends

Take a moment and write down some of your favorite time killers during the work day. The more you can be aware of what you are doing with your time the more you can control it.

The Value of Your Time

I know you've probably done the exercise by which you determine the value of your time. You divide your yearly salary by 2,080 (the number of hours in a 40-hour work week for one year) and come up with the value of each hour. This is most often used to demonstrate that you should only be doing things that are worth that investment in time. There is also a strong suggestion that if it costs less to pay someone to do an activity than your time is worth, you should hire them. For example, if you can pay someone $25 to mow your lawn, which takes you an hour-and-a-half and your time is worth $40 an hour, then you should pay to have it done.

What these calculations never take into account is whether you are in a financial position to pay another person to do the things you don't need or want to do. It also doesn't take into account whether you are willing to make that kind of judgment about your time. You've got to be honest; many of us would not pay someone to pick up our dry cleaning, even if it might be a smart thing to do.

Your time has value beyond the dollars you gain from making your life more manageable. There is no way to pay someone to have the experience of watching your child play or going on vacation with your spouse. Only you can experience those delights. So when you look at the value of your time, the best way to measure is to compare it to what you are trading for the time you are using right now. If you stop taking drop-in visitors during the day and so get to make it to your child's recital on time without feeling guilty, you've created great value. Often, by measuring your time in terms of what you are missing by not actively managing your work time, you find there are more compelling reasons than money to take charge.

Advice from a Sergeant

Dennis Stockwell is a Master Sergeant in the U.S. Army; he's also a former drill sergeant. As a drill sergeant, Dennis controlled every moment of new recruits' time. They didn't have to worry about their time; all decisions were made for them. Now, as a senior supervisor in the military, MSG Stockwell has a very different need for control of time, and he teaches his subordinates valuable lessons.

I asked MSG Stockwell what's the most important thing he's learned in the Army about time, and he said it was "exactly how much can be accomplished in ten minutes." He said that, while the military is still notorious for its hurry-up-and-wait attitude, when it is time to get things done, much can be accomplished in a short time with the right focus. "I have my staff separate activities into glass balls and rubber balls. You can only keep so many balls in the air at a time. If a glass ball falls, you don't get a second chance. If a rubber ball falls it bounces, and you can put it back into play when it comes back up. Focus on managing the glass balls and let the rubber balls bounce; they were not as important in the first place. Put them back into the air at a more appropriate time."

Another interesting observation from MSG Stockwell was his idea of touching things once. "When I watch Privates working, they often move something from one place to another and then have to move it again because

OTHER TIME TIPS FROM DENNIS STOCKWELL

- Schedule expected tasks like checking e-mail or making phone calls at specific times each day.
- Remember that e-mail is a tool, not an emergency. Most people don't need to check e-mail every three or four minutes.
- Be sure you understand your superiors' priorities. Know what they need accomplished and when so that you can effectively manage your time.
- People wait until the last minute to do a task they are unfamiliar with; they stay away from confrontation until it can't be avoided. Plan and prioritize in advance so you can get the information or help you need to complete the task.
- If you are a manager, manage time and prioritize properly by using IPRs, guidance, and milestones. IPRs are In Progress Reviews; review progress regularly yourself and with your staff for maximum success. Give regular guidance to your staff or others whom you rely on for help. Set milestones so you can measure progress and reprioritize or reallocate assets where necessary.
- Create systems wherever possible to speed up and make routine tasks more efficient. Systems are the reason that the Army is able to move massive amounts of troops, equipment, and resources anywhere in the world in a very short period of time. The systems are in place and they've been practiced over and over so that when they count they work.
- Use a calendaring system, whether it is a PDA, BlackBerry, Franklin Planner, or paper calendar; create a time management system that allows you to stay on track.
- Be ruthless in your control of your time.

they didn't take the time to find out where it belonged in the first place. It was an inefficient effort. So, I started training all my staff to only touch things once. Get all the information you need to do the job completely the first time and then complete it. Too much time is wasted in exerting effort to do something half way and then having to recreate the momentum to finish the job. Touching things once saves tremendous amounts of time."

The Secret to Managing Time

The secret to managing time is in the action taken during the time spent on a project. Be focused in your effort. Always attack your task with passion and resolve to give it 100 percent of your effort. If you let your focus waver for even a moment, you kill momentum. Starting momentum takes more effort than keeping it going.

Managing Your Time

Go back to the exercise that we did earlier, in which you wrote down how much time you spent on tasks and compared it to your actual calendar. Take control of the 5s and get rid of as many of the time killers as you can. Harshly evaluate the 4s; do they really need to be done, and by you? Look closely at the 3s; are they really 3s or are they 4s? Examine the 1s and 2s; did they take more or less time than you scheduled? Be conscious of your ability to estimate your time and you'll become more efficient at investing it. Finally, look at the I and D list. Immediately delegate everything you can to another staff person. Set the expectation for what needs to happen and let it the actual work go to someone else.

We all get the same number of minutes in a day; it is up to you how much you get out of each one. By being ruthless in your elimination of interruptions, systematic in your time management, and disciplined in applying your process, you'll accomplish more in every hour of every week than you've ever imagined possible.

One-Hour Action Plan

What Specifically Do I Want to Accomplish?

Take control of my time.

What Specifically Am I Going to Do to Manage My Time?

- Go through the time management exercise for one week and keep track of scheduled time in comparison to the actual use of your time throughout the day.
- Evaluate the information collected from the previous questions and work through the answers to fully understand why you are undertaking this action and what you must do to be successful.
- List the specific steps that are necessary to achieve the desired result.
- Add deadlines to each step.
- Note who will be involved in or responsible for each step if others are to be involved.
- Allocate and schedule the time for this action plan and associated steps to be implemented.
- How will you define success so we know that you've been successful?
- What is the one action step you can take this very moment that will initiate this action plan?

Business Hour 3— Management

Managing is one of the most important requirements of a business owner and one of the last to get focus. It is easy to put actual managing off to focus on other issues. Here's reality: If you spent focused time on managing people, you'd have to deal with fewer issues that require your attention to correct.

Don't confuse managing people with process or project management; they are not the same. In the past, planning, organizing, leading, and controlling were the most important tasks a manager could undertake. Today things are much more complex. In addition to those core competencies, you must focus on ensuring that people who report to you are clear about your vision, your expectations for implementation, and your desired outcome. You must also empower them, and provide them with structure and support while you are creating a vibrant corporate culture. Of these, creating an appropriate culture for people to thrive will produce the biggest and most noticeable results.

Management is creating a vision, setting expectations, and creating an environment for success. The most important thing you can do is have a clear message with measurable milestones that everyone understands and is working toward. Creating an environment for success means giving people clear directions, setting the proper expectations, and holding people accountable for results. You must provide them the support and structure they need to accomplish the goal.

Creating and Articulating Your Vision

Your company can't go where the leader doesn't lead. In order for the company to grow, you have to lead your people toward the goal you want them to help you reach. The only way you can lead and manage effectively is if you know what your real objective is.

General goals like "to be profitable" simply don't work; they are far too undefined to have the possibility of success. You must first clearly decide where you want the business to grow over the next month, year, five years, 10 years, 20 years, and beyond. You also need to be clear how achieving each goal will help you to the next longer-term goal. Each achieved goal should be the platform for goals to come.

In defining your business ask yourself the following questions:

- What is my ultimate goal for the company?
- What is important about that goal?
- What will happen if I don't achieve the goal (if the answer is nothing, you've defined the wrong goal).
- Why am I building this company? (I'm strongly in the camp that says the only reason to build a business is to sell it, because you can't run it forever.)
- What effort and action will it take to reach this goal?
- What commitment do I need from my staff to accomplish this goal?
- How will I know when this goal has been achieved?
- What is in it for all the people who are supporting the goal with me?

- What is the single rallying point for this goal that I can always drive people back to when they are off track, frustrated, or confused?
- What are the simplest terms I can use to communicate my goal and inspire action?
- What can I do to create an environment constantly primed for success?

Here is the single goal that I have for my company: Bold Approach. I manage toward this goal every day, and I make sure that my staff know exactly what they have to do to help me achieve my goal.

THE BOLD APPROACH GOAL

We will be the most recognized and important business growth consultancy to companies with revenues of 1 million to 100 million dollars. We will create a new category by which all future competitors will be judged. That category is called "Business Acceleration Strategy." When privately held businesses in one of our three focus areas find themselves in need of help, they'll only have one choice at the top of their mind at any time and that choice is Bold Approach. Our three focus areas are:

1. Businesses who've recently added a new product or division that needs rapid consumer acceptance.
2. Businesses that have reached a plateau in sales while their market continues to expand around them.
3. Businesses that are in a turn-around situation and need to create rapid revenue generation.

The purpose of our business is to develop a systematic process, detailed strategies, and powerful tactics that can be applied to any of our defined focus areas with minimal customization to achieve rapid profitable results for the client and Bold Approach, Inc. The result of this systemization will be the development of Bold Approach into a company that can be sold for top market value in ten years.

At any given time I can look back at the vision by myself, with managers or with the whole organization, and ask the following questions to see whether we are on track.

- Are we reaching our identified clients?
- Are we creating systemized solutions that have applicability across all of our clients?
- Are the projects we are working on moving us closer to the goal of building a business that can be sold profitably in ten years?
- Based on our vision, should we be working on the projects we are currently working on?
- Do we have the right people in place to accomplish our goals?
- Do we have the culture in place that supports the vision?
- Is our vision still the correct vision?
- Are we achieving success?

By constantly measuring against the management vision it is easy to stay on task and get the job done.

Creating Your Business Culture

Of all the management tasks you can spend time on, creating a culture has to rank near the top of the list. Every organization has a culture, good or bad. Every fast-growing, profitable organization has a thriving culture that seems to have a life of its own but is actually the careful creation of focused management.

Your culture is the living, breathing part of your organization that gives your business palpable energy. It is the sum of all the actions and beliefs you hope to breathe into the entity. Done correctly, it does take on a life of its own that grows and evolves into an integral part of who you are. Done correctly, it leaves your organization and permeates your customers, making them fervent believers in you, your products, and your culture. Some of the most visible cultures that have achieved this level of success are: Apple, Harley-Davidson, Starbucks, Google, and Saturn.

There are literally dozens more exceptional examples that are part of our everyday interaction and lexicon. There are many small to midsized companies that create this kind of enthusiasm every day. They are niche businesses where employees love to work and customers love to buy. Your goal should be to make your business one of those.

Creating an amazing culture in your organization isn't as difficult as it may sound. It is a matter of implementing a few powerful ideas and supporting people in their adaptation.

To start creating a powerful culture, evaluate your existing culture. Look for areas that lack innovation, motivation, and enthusiasm. It is typically not an employee issue that causes those problems; it is lack of appropriate management and focus.

Empower Employees

Empowered employees are the backbone of strong cultures and strong companies. Empowering employees does not mean letting them make any decision they want; it means setting up a structure so they know what decisions they can make, your expectations for their decisions, and your support for them. When they make bad decisions, it means reviewing their decision-making process and helping them understand the impact of what they decided. Help them to understand where the decision got off track, the ramifications of the decision, and how to develop a process toward making better decisions in the future. The final step is allowing them to move forward in their decision-making ability.

Empowerment means trusting qualified people to get the job done while still tracking the milestones. Empowerment is the opposite of micromanagement. By focusing, communicating expectations, setting milestones and then checking them, you allow people the freedom to get the job done. The job doesn't necessarily have to be done the way you would do it, it just needs to be done correctly, efficiently, and on time. Remember, your focus should be on managing the business, not managing individual processes. People who work for you want to feel as if they are contributing to your success and to the success of the business. They want to know that their contribution has meaning and will create a work situation that is good for them.

Motivation and Recognition

One of the techniques I have all my clients use is employee feedback. We do a survey of their employees and have the employees rate their managers and the CEO. We also have managers rate the CEO. It is very interesting to see what comes back in terms of missing skills or perceived lack of focus. Nearly always, the employees are correct.

The deficiency I see most, particularly in companies that don't actively focus on their culture, is lack of recognition. Recognition is closely tied to motivation; people who are recognized feel motivated to do more. They want to participate so that they will get more recognition. Most managers fail in this area because they don't feel they personally need or want recognition for the job they do. The result is that the managers fail to recognize employees regularly who need that recognition.

The best way to recognize people is to do it personally. Walking around the organization and praising people for their success or accomplishments will do more for creating a culture of success than any other thing you can do. If you have a management team assisting you, make it part of their management commitment to point out, every week, employees who deserve recognition. There is nothing better than saying what you think face-to-face, but if the person is far away, send him an e-mail or, better yet, write him a letter or hand-written note and send it to him overnight.

Continue to invest your hours in finding ways to improve your culture. By focusing on developing an internal culture you'll find that employees quickly emulate your example. Once they start to emulate you, your customers will begin to notice. What they'll notice first is the excitement your staff exhibits. The next thing they'll notice is the powerful difference in service and commitment. The final thing they will notice is that they are beginning to understand how they can bring more of what you have into their own organization.

Delegate for Success

The final area you should focus on is your ability to delegate. I have talked about this in Chapter 15, on time management, but it is such a vital management skill that I have to address it here too.

Delegation is a core competency every manager must develop to be successful. As your responsibility grows, you have less time to focus on day-to-day tasks. I can't tell you how many times I've heard managers who are working 18-hour days say, "It is easier to do this myself than to redo it or train someone else to do it."

The only way you can effectively accomplish your goal of growing and building a business is to reduce the dependence of the day-to-day operations on you. Ask yourself this question: "What would happen if I were hospitalized tomorrow and could not do these important tasks. Who would do them? Who else in the organization knows how to do what I'm doing?"

It is dangerous to the long-term health of your business to be the only person who can do what needs to be done to keep the business running. It is also short-sighted if you've hired others to help you but assume they cannot accomplish what needs to be done. Hire the right people, focus on training them, and start delegating. If they get too busy, then you may need to hire someone else or look at who in the organization is next to be trained and delegated to.

People always ask me what the best learning experience I had from the Army was, and there were many. But the thing that really sticks in my mind is how the organization puts tremendous responsibility and expectations on young people. The reason the young people are able to accomplish the assigned tasks is that they know clearly what the expectation is and they are empowered to do it. Every day in the military, men and women under 20 years old handle nuclear weapons, manage air traffic control, keep fleets of vehicles running, and manage all of the human resources of one of the largest employers in the world. They do it effectively, efficiently, and correctly because someone delegated the task to them and expects that it will happen. You can do it too. Your people want to work for you, they want to help, they want to succeed, and they are looking to you to give them the chance. Do it; you'll never be sorry you did.

One way to recognize people is to give them meaningful tasks. Delegation also frees you to work on agendas that make better use of your time. Here is how to delegate simply and easily:

1. *Determine who is best suited to accomplish the task.* If you are worried that your employees are too busy, remember that if it is important enough for you to do it, it is important enough to replace a task on an employee's list. Once you've determined who can accomplish the task, move onto the next step.

2. *Explain the task and expectations in as much detail as necessary.* Demonstrate the expectation of the rest of the business. Determine the standards by which the task will be judged and the milestones by which it will be measured.

3. *Give authority and support.* It is imperative you give the person to whom you are delegating the task the authority to accomplish it. You must also give him the resources necessary to finish the task.

4. *Get positive feedback of understanding and commitment.* It is vitally important that you get feedback from the person to whom you are delegating. He must indicate an understanding of the expec-

tations, the requirements of the task, and willingness to complete it. Do not skip this step; if you do, this is the overriding reason delegated tasks don't get accomplished.

5. *Get out of the way.* Once you've followed the four previous steps, remove yourself and let the task get done. If you start micromanaging or looking over the employee's shoulder, you not only rob him of a feeling of worth and ability, you are wasting your time and reinforcing a wrong expectation. You are also taking away the employee's responsibility for the outcome.

Work on doing little things every day that improve the culture of your company. Every effort has a disproportionately positive and cumulative effect moving forward. Your focus on improving management will improve your organization rapidly, visibly, and profitably.

One-Hour Action Plan

What Specifically Do I Want to Accomplish?

Revitalize my management.

What Specifically Am I Going to Do to Identify the First Area of Focus?

- Evaluate the company culture and develop a plan to improve it.
- Create or reexamine and improve the vision.
- Evaluate the information collected from the previous questions and work through the answers to fully understand why you're undertaking this action and what you must do to be successful.
- List the specific steps necessary to achieve the desired result.
- Add deadlines to each step.

- Note who will be involved in or responsible for each step if others are to be involved.
- Allocate and schedule the time for this action plan and associated steps to be implemented.
- How will you define success so you know you've been successful?
- What is the one action step you can take this moment that will initiate this action plan?

Business Hour 4— Sales and Marketing

I've been heavily involved in consulting with companies that are having financial problems due to changes in their market. What I find nearly every time is that they've lost focus on sales and marketing.

The focus is often lost because managers or business owners don't understand sales and marketing. To many, it is a black art; something that is not easily quantifiable or manageable. They look only at the bottom line and believe that if it's growing, then sales and marketing must be working, and if the bottom line is slipping they believe something has to change. The problem with "something has to change" is that no one really knows what must change.

By spending one hour of Fearsome Focus on your sales and marketing organization, you'll be able to create and renew sources of income that will take your business to a new level. It doesn't matter if you are a sales and marketing manager or a business owner; it is your responsibility to focus on this critical team for an hour and to develop a plan for moving forward.

Here are a few of the things you should be tightly focused on:

- What has changed in the competitive landscape of my industry in the past 12 months?

- What skills are my sales and marketing people missing that would make them more effective?
- What beliefs, about the industry or our company, are held by sales and marketing, the front line of my company?
- What is different about the sales and marketing teams of my competitors compared to my own?
- Why is my top performer so much better than my lowest performer?
- Why is my lowest performer still on the team? (This is a brutal but very powerful question.)
- What is my team better at and worse at than the rest of the industry?
- Who is the formal team leader and who is the informal leader, and which one has the most power over the actions of the team?
- What changes have I put off that need to be made in the sales and marketing organization?
- What is the single most important item I can focus on right now that will have the biggest impact on the team?

By completing that series of questions, you'll begin to get a picture of activity in your teams and you can begin to put together an Achievement Action Plan that allows you to set out goals for change and growth.

In terms of your marketing, there are many questions that need answering in order to create change in the marketplace.

- What are we known for?
- What do we want to be known for?
- What can we say about ourselves that our competition can't say about themselves?
- Are we a marketing-focused company or a product-focused company?
- When was the last time we surveyed our customers and what did they say about us?
- Do we value marketing or look at it as a cost center?

- If we make financial cuts, would marketing be one of the first to go?
- When was the last time we updated our marketing messages?
- What does our competition say that is negative about us but true?
- Can I honestly tell someone in less than 30 seconds what we do and why they should do business with us?

These questions give you tremendous insight into current marketing thinking. If you find yourself saying things like "marketing is a cost center" or "If I had to make financial cuts, marketing would be one of the first to go," then you've got a significant problem in your approach.

Marketing is the lifeblood of every business. If you aren't providing a reason for potential customers to know about you, care about you, and do business with you, your business will fail, no exceptions.

Here is what happens to many companies, especially small and mid-sized ones. There is no focus on measuring marketing results; following the old adage, "Half of my marketing dollars are wasted, I just don't know which half." That is pure insanity in any business and the surest way to financial failure. By positioning your company so it is significantly and specifically separated from your competition, you have the opportunity to gain or regain market share. Customers aren't scrutinizing the differences between you and your competition. Customers want whatever makes their life easiest and makes the most sense to them. Only a small percentage of your potential customers invest any time in comparison shopping. When faced with two similar companies and products, buyers go with the one they have the most experience with, comes recommended, or is most convenient to do business with.

Unique Differentiator

During your Power Hour, analyze your marketing material and make sure the message is a true and unique differentiator. You must present the message so it is relevant to the audience most interested in your product or service.

It's important to remember that longer hours, better selection, and friendly helpful staff are not differentiators. Nearly everyone can say the same about their organizations. If you can quantify what each of those things means, relative to your competition, and quantify what it means to your prospects, they can be a part of your differentiation. If you can't, forget about them; they are meaningless. For example, the big-box stores that successfully outsell many small businesses have done it on those ideals. But what they are missing universally is a well-trained, motivated, and committed staff. That is a significant differentiator if you tell the story in a way that is interesting and relevant. You have to be able to be different in a way that is meaningful and understandable to your customers and them alone. Remember, you are not selling products and services to everyone; you are focused on those customers who have already demonstrated some interest. Stop worrying about all the people who could be your customers and focus on those who should be your customers.

Here are some of the questions you can ask yourself during your hour of focus that will help you understand what your unique difference is:

- What are the most important things that we can do that our competition cannot? How do we know?
- What is the single most important reason, beyond service, that our customers return?
- What does our competition say about themselves that we don't say about ourselves but should?
- Why is what we do important to the customer?
- When confronted with a cheaper price, why do people buy from us anyway?
- What one positive thing would prospects be shocked to know about us?
- What do we take for granted about our product or service?

- What specifically is exceptional about our customer service? Our product? Our staff? Our location? Our Business Model?

- What are our customers surprised that we do? Why are they surprised by it?

- Who are our most significant clients that everyone would know, and what is the story behind why they do business with us instead of our competitors?

- If you could change one thing to make you uniquely different, what would you change?

- What is keeping you from changing it?

- Would the cost or effort involved in changing it be offset quickly by the increase in business it would create?

It is imperative that you think carefully about your answers. Don't just trust your judgment; ask others for their input as well. Ask your customers, your staff, and your past customers who've left you. Once you have a strong feel for what is truly, uniquely different about you, start telling that story and evaluating what happens.

Advertising

Advertising is another area of sales and marketing that needs to be evaluated to make sure it is doing the job needed to keep your business growing. Your advertising is either profitable or not. Building brand awareness can be a good outcome of advertising, but only if it is profitable. Building a brand alone isn't enough. Pets.com was one of the best known brands of the dot-com era, and even to this day many people remember its sock puppet icon because of the effectiveness of the repetition. The company did not survive. Don't focus on building a brand as your primary objective; focus on building a brand people need and will actually spend their money on.

Experience is often overlooked in relation to advertising. If you create compelling advertising and the customer's experience with you is bad, you lose.

I frequently recommend to my clients (and they hate hearing it) to clean up their store, and to train their phone staff to answer the phone in a friendly and helpful manner (I do mean answer and help, not pass people from machine to machine). When organizations start working on creating an experience that customers enjoy, profits increase. People who have positive experiences have higher levels of trust, pay more for the same products, and remain loyal. They are not buying a product, they are buying an experience, an expectation, and the sense of trust that comes with a positive experience. When a business creates the right experience, all other buying expectations in your category will be compared to it. If you create the right experience, your competition won't be able to recreate it and your customers will not feel comfortable buying from them. Make sure your experience is an extension of your advertising. Create the promise of salvation from whatever problem your products or services solve; then give it to them when they arrive.

Here are the most powerful questions to ask about your advertising:

- Does my advertising seek to entertain or to give people facts that drive them closer to a buying decision?
- Does every ad have a call to action? (You can build a brand and ask people to buy at the same time.)
- Are your ads presented with enough frequency to reach the same people often enough to drive your message deep into their long term memory? According to Roy Williams, Wizard of Ads, an ad needs to be heard or seen at least three times in seven nights by the same person to move it from short to long term memory.
- Do your ads sound like every other ad in your category?
- After watching your ad, do you know exactly what you should do next?

- Does your ad have a strong headline or opener that reaches through your prospects' reverie and advertising walls and grabs them by the ears or eyes and compels them to pay attention?
- Is your offer irresistible?
- Is your customer experience nothing short of amazing?
- Are you doing things for your customers your competition would never even consider?
- Are you telling that story in your advertising?
- Does your ad tell a story and build on earlier stories that you've told?
- Do you measure your advertising results?

Public Relations

If you are not maximizing your public relations activities, you are missing one of the most lucrative new prospect opportunities available. Done correctly, PR is a client-generating gold mine. There is one simple reason that PR is so effective. It is a third party endorsement by a trusted source in a place where we expect to learn about the latest information and ideas. Quite simply, we trust the news and the people who deliver it.

Many companies issue one or two boring media releases a year without thinking about what it might do for them if they were to tell a real story. They also miss the opportunity that media releases have to create a tsunami of web traffic that can easily be monetized.

Here is the harsh reality about PR. Editors are people too. They are pressured, over-worked, curious, under constant deadlines and always in need of new stories and sources. If they don't get those new stories and sources, they have to fall back on updating the stories that they had or using the same old sources because they are reliable. If you know that and take advantage of it, there is no reason you can't get all the published stories you want.

When I owned a used computer store, I had a great relationship with a local editor and I gave her at least 10 story ideas and sources each week. Most of these were not stories about computers but business stories that were interesting and compelling. About once a week a story that I had suggested was in the paper. About once a month, I was quoted in some other business article, and I was always identified as the owner of the local computer store. People wanted to do business with me because they felt that I was well known and knowledgeable since my name was in the paper all the time. My business flourished because I knew how to use PR.

Ask yourself these questions:

- What have we done that is interesting lately that we haven't told the media about? Be sure you don't forget about hiring new employees or winning new contracts.
- What stories are currently in the news that we can tie into or comment on?
- What unique information do we have that a reporter would be interested in knowing?
- Can we write a tip sheet or special consumer awareness report with seven to 10 things that every consumer should know before buying products or services in our category? The media are always looking for tips and checklists that they can use in support of their stories.
- Are we distributing our releases through online resources like PRWEB.com to ensure that we are being seen online and that we are getting valuable links back to our site?
- Do we have an online PR strategy that allows us to link our most important keywords back to us to increase our site visitors?
- Is the person who is in charge of our PR adequate for the job? Does he or she know all the key journalists covering our industry?

- Do we send releases to the media with no journalist contact prior to sending?
- Do we follow up with the journalists that the release was sent to in order to be sure that they received it?
- Do we treat our PR process the same way we treat our sales lead follow-up? (If not, you should; follow-through in person or by phone is crucial to being covered regularly.)
- Do we have a personal relationship with the top 25 journalists in our industry or who cover us?
- Do we know which media coverage gets the most response for us?
- Do we have a plan for what to do with the coverage we get?

If you answered no to many of the questions, you may find that focusing clearly on media during a one-hour focus time will result in a tremendous increase in the coverage you receive. Virtually anyone can get covered by the media if they take the time to focus and create a real reason for the media to be interested.

One-Hour Action Plan

Armed with your new information, let's turn it into a One-Hour Action Plan that you can use to transform your team.

What Specifically Am I Going to Accomplish?

Increase the productivity and profitability of my sales and marketing organization.

What Specifically Am I Going to Do to Increase Their Productivity and Profitability?

- Define what an increase in productivity means and how you'll measure it.
- Define how much of an increase in profitability you want and how it will be measured, as well as how often.
- Evaluate the information you collected from the previous questions for the biggest opportunities and implement those.
- List the specific steps that are necessary to achieve the desired result.
- Add deadlines to each step.
- Note who will be involved in or responsible for each step.
- Allocate and schedule the time for this action plan and associated steps to be implemented.
- How will you define success so we know that you've been successful?
- What is the one action step you can take this very moment that will initiate this action plan?

As you go through this chapter again doing the exercises, I hope you'll find dozens of more powerful questions both critical and creative that you can ask yourself. If you'll constantly ask more and better questions about your sales and marketing opportunities, you'll continually improve and find competitive advantage long before your competition even begins to catch up.

Business Hour 5— Customer Experience

In Chapter 17 I touched on customer experience, which is so important it needs a full chapter to better explain the process. I want you to focus on customer experience with such intensity that an outsider looking in would say you are obsessed. In my opinion, when you are obsessed with your customer experience, you are close to the real breakthrough that will endear customers to you forever. You create a cult following that couldn't be pried away from you with the world's biggest crowbar.

The reason that customer experience is so important is pretty simple. Companies try to copy everything they can about one another, and in some cases that is a very good thing for the company and the consumer. The problem is that once companies in the same category start copying each other, they become similar in many ways. The more similar companies become, the less loyal a customer needs to be because there is less and less difference to pay attention to. Look at the big-box technology stores. It is very difficult to tell whether you are in CompUSA, Best Buy, or Circuit

City. In fact, in many cases if they didn't have their signage and logos everywhere, you'd have a hard time telling the three apart. If you can't tell them apart, how can they ever hope to make you a loyal fan? They can't even rely on price any more. Wal-Mart can probably beat any of them and if not, they'll kill loyalty by beating their competitor's price. They actually encourage people not to be loyal but to be price shoppers instead.

But the problem goes much deeper. What I described is not just their process; it is the customer's experience when they go into the store. They know they can get a better deal at the competitor's store, and they use that information to negotiate a better deal where they are. They know they are getting basic information that is questionably valid at any of the stores where they shop, so they do their research before they hit the door. And, the minute they walk through the door of any of the big stores or big consumer outlets (cell phone companies like Cingular are notorious), they are met by employees who act eager to help until you ask too many questions and then they can't be through with you fast enough.

Compare that to companies that focus on creating a memorable customer experience every time. Westin hotels are a perfect example. When you go to a Westin, you know you'll get impeccable service. Shoe shines are free and someone picks the shoes up from your room and delivers them back when shined. Need anything? Call service express and your request will be taken care of. They follow up with a call to make sure everything is satisfactory. Turn-down service? Yes, every night, with two chocolates left on your pillow. Comfortable beds? Their heavenly beds are so comfortable you can buy one from their company catalog. Not to mention robes in every room, a cordless phone, and wireless internet. Now that is an experience worth paying a little more for. There are plenty of hotels with cheaper rooms that have comfortable beds and good service, but the experience that you get at the Westin is memorable. You compare every other hotel you stay in to the experience you had there. You tell people about it, you can't help it.

In a moment, I'm going to walk you through a series of questions that will help you create a very unique customer experience. Before I do, I want you to ask yourself this question: Is it possible to create an experience in our organization that is so unique that our clients can't wait to tell others about it? Virtually anyone reading this book should be able to say yes, but if you can't yet, you will be able to in just a moment.

What are people looking for in an experience and what can make it unique? In your particular business or industry there will be other things quite obvious to you that your clients want, but from a macro level, here they are:

- To be catered to.
- To get accurate, helpful information.
- To not be pressured but to have questions answered.
- To be given help in making an appropriate decision.
- To be treated to a level of service unexpected in your category of business.
- To be surprised by at least one or two things that make the experience exciting.
- To be able to have access to someone who can answer questions quickly.
- To be treated with dignity and respect.
- To have salespeople be genuinely curious about their needs and wants.
- To be heard.
- To be reassured.
- To be inspired.
- To be educated.
- To be given room when they want it and help the instant they need it.
- To feel comfortable that they are getting great value for their money.
- To know that the level of service they receive today will be the same the next time they come in, even if they come back with a problem.

- To be recognized when they are a frequent buyer.
- To feel like they have some level of relationship to the people they are spending their money with.

If you'll apply this simple list of expectations to your environment, you'll increase your sales and profitability overnight. Here are a few things I've used with companies, large and small, to instantly increase sales:

- Get rid of phone automation and have a live person answer the phone.
- Clean the bathrooms in a professional services organization.
- Have everyone start wearing uniforms so they are easy to spot in crowds of people.
- Have a greeter shake everyone's hand who comes through the door and ask his name, then introduce him to a salesperson.
- Give everyone walking through the door a cold bottle of water in the summer and a cup of hot chocolate in the winter. Another company gives chocolates to everyone who comes in.
- Require the first person the customer interacts with when reporting a problem to stay on the phone until the customer is transferred to someone who can solve his problem; then have the first person call back after the consultation is complete to be sure that the customer was well served. The final step is to send an e-mail with the solution to the problem so that they have a record of how to fix the problem if it recurs. The e-mail contains information about the solution, either in written format or an MP3 recording of the actual call solving the problem.

Those are just a few things that have been done with hundreds of different companies. What can you do with your company to create an experience that will make customers want to return?

Finding Our Exceptional Experience

Ask yourself the following questions and be sure you write down the answers. Remember, your experience doesn't have to be hundreds of times better (though it is nice if it is) than that of your competition; it just needs to be memorable and compelling.

- What do we currently do that is probably a little annoying to customers and how can we change it?
- What do we do currently that customers find very helpful?
- What could we easily do that our clients would not expect but that would enhance their experience with us?
- What could we do that our competition would never do that would make our clients tell their friends about their experience?
- What is one thing our sales staff could do to make the sales process simpler and more personal?
- If your primary interaction with clients is over the phone, how can you make that experience even more pleasant and simple?
- If your primary interaction is over the phone, where is the bottleneck in the system? How can you correct it and improve the experience?
- If your primary interaction is in person, what can you do to better welcome people and get them engaged in the experience they have with you?
- If you are interacting in an office or building, what needs to be cleaned, updated, moved, or discarded to make the atmosphere more inviting and exciting?
- Can you better train your staff on the products or services you sell so the information they give matches or exceeds the information that the prospects may have when they first connect with you?
- What can you do to improve your customer service?
- How can you lay out your store or office to make it more inviting? (Think about dentists' offices; they used to be very sterile and clinical

and now they may look out into a garden and have a television in the ceiling for you to watch while you block out any noise with headphones.)

- Which of your people consistently please your clients and which ones don't? What do they do differently?
- What do your clients wish they could find or that would happen in terms of the store experience? If you listen to what they say and implement it, they'll reward you with their loyalty and word-of-mouth advertising.
- What drives you nuts about your current experience that you imagine probably drives your clients nuts too? Now, fix it.

Pay close attention to your own experiences. If you yourself get frustrated when you can't talk to a live person, and yet you make your clients talk to automation, that may not be a good choice. Your reactions to how you are treated by companies will be similar to those of your clients when confronted with the same experience or behavior.

By taking the time to create a perfect customer experience you'll develop a loyal following that wants to do business with you. Your raving fans will find new ways to do that because they crave the experience more than the products themselves.

Creating a perfect customer experience will be a defining moment in your success that you can look back on. If you are a leader, manager, salesperson, or spouse, what can you do to create an amazing experience when people interact with you? Apply the same concepts and watch your personal following grow!

One-Hour Action Plan

What Specifically Do I Want to Accomplish?

Create an amazing customer experience.

What Specifically Am I Going to Do to Create an Amazing Customer Experience?

- Define what constitutes an amazing customer experience and how you'll measure it.
- Evaluate the information I collected from the previous questions for the best ideas and implement those.
- List the specific steps that are necessary to achieve the desired result.
- Add deadlines to each step.
- Note who will be involved in or responsible for each step.
- Allocate and schedule the time for this action plan and associated steps to be implemented.
- How will you define success so we know that you've been successful?
- What is the one action step you can take this moment that will initiate this action plan?

Business Hour 6— Making Connections

What I'm going to say in the next paragraph will anger some of you but that's okay; you need to hear it and you need to consider it.

Connections are the lifeblood of business but not all connections are equal. In business the ultimate purpose of making connections is to develop a more profitable business through increased revenue or information sharing. There is no other functional purpose for developing connections in business. You may ultimately end up with some new friends from these connections, but that is not the reason for developing them.

While nearly every senior executive, business owner, or salesperson knows the value of networking, few do it regularly or correctly. Networks are most often neglected for two reasons. First, because we often falsely assume that once we've made a connection we will always have it. Connections, like gardens must be tended. Second, we fall prey to the idea that "we have enough friends already." Business is about connections and not about friends. The best businesses in the world are built on millions of connections.

The time I schedule each week for maintaining connections never gets bumped. Over the years, by necessity, I've expanded my hour to two hours per week because of the size of the network I've developed. During those hours I apply Fearsome Focus to connecting and furthering relationships.

Knowing how to use your network and what you can expect from the different players in your network is important to successful connecting.

Three Types of Connections

- *Mastermind Partners.* This is the top level of connections. Napoleon Hill introduced the idea of Mastermind groups in his classic book called "Think and Grow Rich." Masterminds are small groups of tightly connected individuals who meet on a regular basis for the purpose of moving each other's businesses forward. Typically in these groups, business owners bare their souls and their private business details in order to benefit others in the group, with the expectation that the others will do the same. A great deal of business is referred back and forth.

- *Power Partners.* Power Partners are the people with whom you are connected for the purpose of sharing high level information, leads, joint venture opportunities, and the hope of potentially evolving into Mastermind Partners. Your Power Partners tend to be those people who have significant financial value to you, and vice versa. They are people who can and will open doors and for whom you'll make introductions, recommendations, and endorsements. An additional classifier for these people is "business friends."

- *Casual Connections.* Casual Connections have potential value in terms of business connections. They are also those people who may have been Power Partners at one time but have moved to a different position or company and don't have the same value in terms of connections. You want to keep up with them in case they move back into your industry or their status changes in some important way. An additional classifier for these people is "business acquaintances."

In order to better understand each connection, how to develop it, and what to expect from it, let's look at each connection in more detail.

Mastermind Partner

The Mastermind Partner is the highest level partner because they are actively involved in the success of your business or career. These are people you meet with on a regular basis in order to share challenges, successes, and opportunities. They are people you share your advice and connections with to help them achieve their goals, and visa versa. These people are almost never in an industry or business competitive to you because of the information you'll share.

Mastermind Partners most often evolve and develop out of the Power Partner relationship, when one of you decides that a more formal structure to your relationship would be mutually beneficial and suggests it. You are virtually never able to break into a Mastermind group simply by knowing of its existence and asking to join. You either create the group and invite like-minded individuals or you are recommended to the group by another of your connections.

You can expect great things from good Mastermind Partners. Mastermind Partners are all focused on providing information, contacts, insight, ethical and legal insider views into industries, companies, or pieces of business. Your Mastermind Partners are a priority to you and you are a priority to them.

Mastermind Partners will endorse you, recommend you, and sell you better than you can sell yourself in many cases. Because the stated intent of the relationship is to advance each other's business, it is understood that this is what will happen. Mastermind Partners are almost fraternal in their connection.

You can ask for and expect to get help, favors (where appropriate and legal), and first consideration for bidded business from the partner's company as it relates to your industry. You can also expect to get an insider's view of how your partners' businesses run, how they make decisions, and the results of those decisions in quantifiable terms. You can expect trust, confidentiality, and a very reciprocal type of relationship.

Power Partners

Power Partners are the business connections you make for the purpose of developing more business. They also develop you to help them. It is a symbiotic relationship that everyone understands. There is an element of friendship in the relationships and a fair amount of sharing that happens in terms of what is going on in each other's organization. There is never complete sharing because often these partners will have multiple connections in a competitive category, so information has to be more general.

You develop Power Partners by initiating a conversation about how you may be able to help each other. You'll can do this through everyday interactions with people in your industry, including vendors, clients, and prospects. You'll also seek out partners actively by studying the key players in your industry and approaching them directly with a value proposition that gives them good reason to engage with you. Power Partners have to be "sold" on the value of the relationship in the beginning. Let me share an example of how this occurs.

John Klymshyn is the author of *Move The Sale Forward*, one of the best sales books ever written and one I highly recommend. I first met John when I interviewed him for a radio program I hosted. John was knowledgeable, interesting, and willing to share information openly. After the broadcast interview, John and I spoke and agreed that there might be ways our businesses could interact profitably. We stayed in touch on a regular basis and I put John's interview on my web site because I felt it was valuable (it is still there).

About four months ago John called to tell me someone had listened to the interview, contacted him, and bought his book. We decided we could help each other increase business. John introduced me to several organizations that needed speakers and I introduced him to my editor so that he could pitch a book, which was ultimately accepted.

Our Power Partner relationship continued to grow and we shared more information about our businesses, our strategies, and our goals for the future. We shared more leads, more business, and more opportunities. We eventually developed a sales training program called "Sales Torque™" and will present it worldwide.

As our relationship developed, I decided John should belong to one of my most important Mastermind Partner groups, so I endorsed him to the group and, with their acceptance, invited him to join.

Before my relationship with John evolved into a Mastermind partnership, his advice, connections, endorsements, and recommendations were worth thousands of dollars to me.

You can expect Power Partners to recommend business to you, make introductions to other influential people, and on occasion endorse you. You cannot reasonably expect Power Partners to exclude competitive relationships. You can expect that Power Partners will help you if they believe it is a reciprocal arrangement where they get something in return for helping you.

You should have more Power Partners than either of the other two groups. Power Partners should also contain your most trusted advisors: your accountant, banker, physician, and attorney, for example.

Casual Connections

Casual Connections are those that may evolve into more meaningful relationships or that may have a limited possibility for mutual benefit. Often these connections are made for a single purpose. For example, I currently use a pediatrician that came highly recommended. I do a lot to try to help her business. She knows very little about mine, nor does she do anything to promote it, and I don't expect that. I like her to be focused on the health of my child. But, I also like knowing she is not taking new patients, and the only way you can get in to her is through a very impassioned recommendation from an existing patient.

Once my daughter is old enough not to need a pediatrician, I'll maintain the relationship because I'll always know people who are having children, and I like being able to reliably recommend the best pediatrician in my area and know that she'll always take people I recommend.

Casual Connections are typically developed through business meetings, casual introductions, or cold calls. Occasionally they are recommendations from Power Partners or Mastermind Partners for specific needs. The relationship is maintained either in order to reciprocate at some point or because it may prove useful in the future. It does not warrant the time investment that will go into the previous two partner relationships. Former clients often fall into the casual connection category.

Maintaining Connections

By far the best book ever written on networking is called *Never Eat Alone*, by Keith Ferrazzi (Currency, 2005). The book contains dozens of great ways to segment your connections and to stay connected. I strongly recommend this book for broadening your thinking horizons.

I'm going to share with you a plan that helps you stay connected quickly and easily, and typically takes you less than an hour a week. Here's why this program takes so little time. First, you'll always have regular contact with your Mastermind Partners so you don't have to stay in touch beyond your current schedule. Power Partners will take up most of your time because of the large number of them. You'll want to contact your Power Partners at least once a month for the purpose of staying connected beyond whatever other contact you may have had with them. Casual Connections are contacted two or three times a year to keep the relationship alive and moving forward. Any relationship that goes more than a year without a connection is not one that can be relied on or that is likely to survive in a meaningful way. After a year the connection may remember who you are, but any reason he or she had to maintain the relationship has probably gone away.

Connecting

Mastermind Partners

Because of the frequency and depth of the contact you have with Mastermind Partners, it is important to connect with them in a personal way a couple of times a year. Some of the best times to connect are birthdays, significant events in the partner's life, or on New Year's Day. For Mastermind Partners, one of your connections should be one-on-one and in person. Dinner, lunch, the theater, a sporting event, or any other occasion can be a great time to connect in person. It is also very helpful to get spouses or significant others involved in the personal meetings whenever possible, to deepen the relationship further. Typically, people who are Mastermind Partners could definitely be considered friends. If you choose to send gifts as a way of connecting with these very important people, be sure that your gift reflects some knowledge of the person. Don't send them the same gift you send everyone else. Make it personal or don't send it at all.

Power Partners

Power Partners should be contacted at least once a month. The best way to connect is by e-mail or phone. E-mail can be a great connector once in a while, but it is no substitute for a phone call or occasional face-to-face meeting. You should always call Power Partners on their birthdays, when they appear in the media (unless it is a daily occurrence; then only on an important occasion), or whenever you have an opportunity to share with them. Be sure that you don't connect with them only when you need something, which is the fastest way to destroy a relationship.

With Power Partners you want your communications to most frequently have a business-related purpose. My recommendation is to contact them twice with an opportunity for them, each time you want something from them. You may find you are in such regular contact with some Power Partners that making an extra effort to stay in touch is not necessary. In those cases, simply make an effort that is personal and not related to business three or four times per year.

Casual Connections

When making contact with your Casual Connections, phone is by far the most important tool. Because these people are out of regular touch with you, they need the element of human contact in order to maintain the relationship. Again, birthdays are always a good choice or, at minimum, the week of their birthday if you know it. If you don't, then pick another meaningful event like New Year's, Christmas, first day of spring, or anything that you can use to build on. You should also contact them with leads when they seem appropriate, or other opportune times such as when they are promoted or featured in the media.

Here is what my personal plan looks like each week.

Daily Personal Plan

Ten Minutes—Birthday or other meaningful day calls for my Power Partners. My message is very simple: "Hi Tim, I know today is your birthday and I wanted to wish you the best birthday ever. I can't believe a year has passed since we met. I hope you'll be doing something very exciting today to celebrate. I know a million people will be calling you, so I won't take up any more of your time. Have a *superb* birthday." In ten minutes I can typically make five of these calls, since most of them will end up going to voice mail anyway. I'll often get a phone call back from at least one person, and I'll have a five-minute conversation with him and make the connection.

Weekly Personal Plan

Tuesdays are my days for connecting. I do 10 calls in 60 minutes, which gives me six minutes per call, and that's plenty. Either I have a reason for calling or, if I don't, I tell them I'm calling to check in because we haven't spoken for a while. I've found that by using a contact manager you never have to wonder what you last spoke about if you take time to jot down notes from each conversation. You can always follow up, or ask questions. I choose Tuesdays because experience has taught me that I will reach more people on that day.

Lately I've been using another tool called Audio Generator. Audio Generator lets me record a single audio message that can be broadcast to many people simultaneously through e-mail. I like Audio Generator because it allows you to connect by voice, without having to go through voice mail or call screeners. Most people will listen because the audio postcard is unique. The tool alone creates many call backs simply because people are curious about it. In fact, if you send me an e-mail at powerofanhour@aweber.com, I'll send you an audio postcard so you can see how it works.

Connecting is not difficult if you discipline yourself to do it. It is one of the most profitable new habits you'll ever develop. One caveat: be sure you are good at wrapping up conversations in a timely manner. Connecting is not an opportunity to waste your day; it is an opportunity to move a relationship forward and to keep each other focused on what the other needs or wants.

This focused hour per week nets me at least 520 connections per year. Answer this next question honestly: Are you currently making 520 connections per year with separate individuals who are your Power Partners? Most people will answer no, and the real number of unique connections will be under 100.

Letting Relationships Die

At some point you'll realize that some business relationships no longer serve a purpose and you need to let them go. In the beginning this is tough to do because we've been taught to maintain relationships. Remember this: You are doing the other person a favor by being the one to let an unproductive relationship die, because then the person won't feel obligated to return your calls or e-mails.

Since there is no possible way to attend properly to every connection we ever make, we have to let some of them go. I strongly encourage you to cull your business relationships today by asking the following questions:

- What is the purpose for staying in touch with this person?
- Have I provided him any information of value in the past year?
- Has he provided me with any connections of value in the past year?
- Am I just going through the motions in this relationship?

- What are three valid reasons for maintaining this relationship for another three months?
- What is the most likely outcome of letting this relationship die?
- Is there any compelling reason to continue to put energy into this relationship?
- Would my time be better used replacing this relationship with a more valuable one?

Remember, connections are the lifeblood of your business. Be sure you invest your time and commitment to them wisely.

One-Hour Action Plan

What Specifically Do I Want to Accomplish?

Improve my connections.

What Specifically Am I Going to Do to Segment and Improve My Current Connections?

- Break my connections into the three defined categories: Mastermind Partners, Power Partners, Casual Connections.
- Evaluate the information collected from the previous questions and work through the answers to fully understand why I am taking this action and what I must do to be successful.
- List the specific steps that are necessary to achieve the desired result.
- Add deadlines to each step.
- Note who will be involved in or responsible for each step if others are to be involved.

- Allocate and schedule the time for this action plan and associated steps to be implemented.
- How will you define success so we know that you've been successful?
- What is the one action step you can take this very moment that will initiate this action plan?

Business Hour 7— Mentoring

One of the best and most fulfilling hours you'll ever spend in business is the hour per week you should spend mentoring someone. You'll not only create a person who is more valuable to your organization, you'll create a better organization. An added benefit of mentoring someone is that you get a view of the organization uniquely different from yours. Seeing your company or department through new eyes can be helpful.

Mentoring is not as hard as a lot of people think. First, let's take a look at what mentoring is and isn't.

Mentoring Is:

- A one-on-one relationship focused on developing another person for advancement in your organization or their career.
- A time for you to openly and candidly share personal experiences as a learning example.
- An opportunity to instill your most important values in another person.

- An opportunity to help construct a more productive employee.
- A chance to leave a legacy in your company or department.
- An opportunity to give someone a valuable training opportunity you likely never got.

Mentoring Is Not:

- A power play.
- A chance to create a clone.
- Done for selfish, greedy reasons or in hopes of personal gain from another person.
- A chance to practice favoritism.
- A chance to demonstrate your power or authority.
- An excuse to spend more time with a friend or buddy at work.
- A chance to find a romantic relationship.

In a mentoring relationship, it is inevitable that friendships will evolve. It is imperative that you don't let that friendship impact your expectations of the person being mentored in a negative way. Your expectations of the person need to remain in line with his or her position and ability. The friendship should not evolve to the point that the person is given unfair advantage or consideration over other, equally qualified people. Mentored people should not get advantages beyond their capability simply because they've been mentored.

Whom Should You Mentor?

In fairness to you, not everyone deserves to be or is capable of being mentored by you. There are typically three kinds of people that are good mentoring candidates. The first is someone who is new to the department or organization and who needs some additional attention in order to get up to speed quickly. This is typically a short-term arrangement.

The second is someone who is being groomed for a position similar to yours. You are a manager and you are mentoring a management candidate, for example. This is typically a long-term commitment to developing skills, knowledge, and organizational ability.

The third mentoring candidate is someone you are mentoring to take your position. This is a midrange kind of relationship, and of the three it is the most potentially damaging to your ego. If this person is more success-ful than you have been in the same position, your ego may be hurt. If the person is less successful, your ego may also be impacted because you feel as if you failed him.

How to Choose Whom You Mentor

If you don't have a formalized mentoring program, there are some fairly simple guidelines you can use to find good mentoring candidates.

- Often, mentoring candidates will identify themselves; they'll let you know when they are ready to be mentored and ask for help.
- You notice a deficiency that needs to be corrected.
- You identify a star performer who needs some additional attention in order to reach his or her maximum potential.
- A recommendation comes from staff or management.

Making Mentoring Work

For a mentoring relationship to work, it must be formalized with commit-ment on both sides. You must identify specific and measurable outcomes expected. You'll use these outcomes to determine the effectiveness of the program. Finally, you have to know when to quit mentoring.

Formalizing the Relationship

The most effective way to formalize the relationship is to have an organized conversation. During the conversation you should ask detailed questions in reference to the candidate's desire and commitment. Here are a few questions you'll want to ask:

What is the most important thing you want from this relationship? The person being mentored should be able to easily answer the question with specific feedback about what he or she believes the outcome should be. As long at the candidate can articulate the outcome and it is on track, the answer is sufficient.

How will you know you are making progress in the relationship? The persons being mentored should be able to help define several milestones used to measure success. They should give you specific examples of skills or experience they will gain to demonstrate competence. Don't expect their answers to be completely formed; you'll have to help make their responses realistic, and you should. Formalizing expectations is a significant key to mentoring success.

What are a candidate's expectations of you in this relationship? They should be able to explain their expectations. You may need to fine tune their expectations to be sure they are in line with what you are willing and able to do.

How much time can you realistically commit to this relationship and still maintain your daily job expectations? The candidate's should give you some indication of how much time they can invest. If all of their time has to come during working hours, it may be difficult to adequately mentor them unless you are willing to commit your own work hours to their advancement. Typically, mentoring relationships will require extra effort and time from both parties.

To finalize the relationship, you should set out your expectations. They need to be clear, concise, and in line with the ability of the person you are helping. Just because you used to put in 18 hours a day when you first started working doesn't mean they should.

Once you've set your expectations, outline a plan of action. Let the person know exactly what to expect. Let him see a plan that will demonstrate how he will progress and what he will need to do and accomplish. Because a mentoring relationship is one where someone is learning new skills, you need to set clear guidelines for your availability. Be sure the mentoring relationship remains a student–teacher relationship and not a crutch for the person you are mentoring.

Creating Commitment on Both Sides

The most important aspect of creating commitment is to actually schedule time to work together. Too often, mentoring someone really means the person is given more work with no interaction. Find a time that both of you can work together, ideally uninterrupted. Schedule time and commit to it. If you must reschedule, it must be rescheduled within the same week.

Setting quantifiable goals also demonstrates commitment on both sides. The commitment starts with you by setting out the goals and continues with their achievement.

Follow through. Commitment is demonstrated by taking the actions each of you promised. Measure your success by your milestone goals.

Developing the Person You Mentor

The goal of mentoring is to develop the person you are working with to be a more effective employee or candidate for a position. Because you have superior knowledge, it is up to you to define the following areas as they relate to your business and the person you are working with. Be sure you are as detailed as possible when you define the areas.

- Job skills
- Management skills
- Personal traits (i.e., communication skills, dress, etc.)
- Company knowledge
- Product knowledge
- Personal skills (writing, speaking, etc.)

Transferring your knowledge is the most important task you'll undertake. The idea is not to make the other person your clone, but to pass on your most valuable skills and allow the person to develop skills of his own. You want new skills to become part of who a person is, not define him.

Be sure you've clearly defined how you'll pass on the skills. The most effective way is through a combination of theory, example, and hands-on experience. People cannot effectively learn a new skill until they understand it fundamentally, see it in action, and then have a chance to put it into action themselves and get positive feedback.

Think of this process as if you were teaching a child to ride a bike. You'd tell the child how it should be done, and why you ride a bike the way you do. You'd then show the child how to do it, and finally you'd get him on the bike and guide him while he learned the new skill. Once he understands the basics, you'd let go of him but still be there to catch him if he fell. Gradually you allow the child to get further and further away, giving him the chance to succeed or fail on his own. You'll be there to give feedback and help if he needs it. Eventually you'll be able to let him go alone. He will still occasionally crash but it will happen with less frequency. Being a mentor is exactly the same.

Your communication needs to be clear and concise with a focus on providing a step-by-step plan for learning a new skill and achieving success. In the mentoring relationship it will be up to you to flex your teaching style to the mentee's learning style for maximum effectiveness.

Once you've transferred a skill and the mentees have learned it well enough to try on their own, let them go. Give them a task or project that requires them to use the newfound skill. Continue this process of learning until you are confident all of the original goals of the mentoring relationship have been met.

Ending the Relationship

Ending a mentoring relationship is a hard thing to do. If you've been a good mentor you'll have developed a relationship and a bond. But, like letting children leave home, you have to cut their reliance on you. You have to let them get their own experience and grow into their new skills. If you've done a good job as a mentor it will show.

The best way to end a relationship is to do it formally. I like to have a dinner with important staff, spouses, or significant others and anyone else from the organization that should be involved. During the dinner, usually between drinks and the entrée, I announce to the group that I've been mentoring a certain person and that over the past months he has grown and achieved new career heights. I let the group know I have high expectations for the mentee and that I am sure he will be effective in any future position. I repeat my strong endorsement of this person.

I've found by having that kind of closure to the relationship there are never any misunderstandings or hard feelings. The person being mentored doesn't feel like he has lost favor because you start mentoring someone else. He feels that he has accomplished something important and that he will always have a resource no matter where he ends up. Everyone remembers his first mentor and rarely loses touch. Mine was Shawn Lee, and I deeply appreciate everything he did to help me set my course early on. The lessons he taught me still serve me well today.

One-Hour Action Plan

What Specifically Do I Want to Accomplish?

Mentor a staff member.

What Specifically Am I Going to Do to Effectively Mentor a Member of My Staff?

- Identify a mentor candidate.
- Evaluate the information collected from the previous questions and work through the answers to fully understand why I am undertaking this action and what must be done to be successful.
- List the specific steps that are necessary to achieve the desired result.
- Add deadlines to each step.
- Note who will be involved in or responsible for each step if others are to be involved.
- Allocate and schedule the time for this action plan and associated steps to be implemented.
- How will you define success so we know that you've been successful?
- What is the one action step you can take this very moment that will initiate this action plan?

Business Hour 8— Give Something Back

Giving back is something we probably all want to do but one of the last things we get around to. It is important to give back to your community or humanity in order to feel the accomplishment that comes from working to solve something bigger than yourself.

Giving back has powerful ramifications on your business and your personal life. While I'm covering giving back as part of your business hours, it could just as easily be covered in the personal hours. I chose to put it in the business hours because in business you have many opportunities to give back that you don't in your personal life. Your resources are different, your opportunities are different, and they are more powerful.

The reason that giving back is so important in business is this. You have the opportunity on a daily basis to create a better life based on your effort and the efforts of those people who work with you. Your profitability comes from your ability to influence others to buy your products or services, and as a result you prosper. No matter where your station in life started, you are now where you are. Whether or not you worked your fingers to the bone to get there, along the way someone helped you, knowingly or unknowingly. Someone gave you a chance, and many people whom you know and don't know are still responsible for your success today.

There are many people in the world who are literally dying in their struggle to have the same chance you have had. Others are literally dying in an effort to get an education. There are others who are close to dying, but struggling to stay alive long enough for someone like you to create a cure for their disease. All of these people need your help. Of course there are many others who need help—those impacted by natural disasters, wars, and any of the other devastations that can be rained down on them at any time.

The bottom line is that you can help. My friend John Forde (www.jackforde.com) writes a wonderful newsletter about copywriting which he could easily charge hundreds of dollars a year for, but he gives it away to help others. That isn't the greatest part of what he does. Inside each letter he names a charity that is looking for someone to write copy to help them raise money. These are typically not huge charities; they are the smaller ones that do all the work they can on a limited budget. John is able to give back in two ways: He gives freely of his knowledge so that you can gain a skill, and then he gives you an opportunity to practice that knowledge by helping someone who needs it.

Too often we believe the only way to help a charity is to write a check. Of course money helps, but writing a check is never as fulfilling as extending a hand to help. It is good for you and it is good for the charity.

When I was young we were dirt poor and, because I was raised in a cult, we were not allowed to celebrate Christmas. One year I was home watching my younger brothers when a car pulled into our driveway. A man pulled out a huge box of presents and food and came to our door. He said he was there to deliver Christmas. I told him we didn't celebrate Christmas and that we didn't accept charity (my mom would have no part of it). He said something to me that I've never forgotten: "Son, this isn't charity, and if you can't celebrate Christmas that is okay. You can give these gifts to someone else who needs them more than you. And, when you get older, you do this for someone who needs something more than you and you'll pay me back. This isn't charity; it is a loan that I expect you to re-pay." He shook my hand, then left the box and drove away without telling me his name. I've paid him back dozens of times over the years. Every time I do, I feel great knowing that someone else will have the chance to do the same. I'm honoring the memory of a man I never knew, setting an exam-ple, and laying out the challenge for someone else I don't know. I am sure some of those people will find better circumstances and they'll ultimately repay me by helping someone else. That is what I want you to do during your hour of giving back. Find a way, a cause, a person, a group, a charity, but find someone who needs your help, and get involved.

Jerome Eberharter is the CEO of White Cloud Coffee, (www.white cloudcoffee.com) and he is passionate about three things: coffee, riding motorcycles, and reading. Jerome decided to give back, and he created his own charity called Ride 2 Read (www.ride2read.org). Every year he hosts a motorcycle rally and raises money to support small libraries across Idaho in an effort to help children and adults learn to read. Do you think that his charitable effort is a challenge for him? Absolutely not—he made it fun, he made it personal, and he is passionate about getting involved. In fact, if you want to take your first step toward charity, make a small donation at www.ride2read.org right now.

Here are a few ways you can give back as a business:

- Donate your employees to a worthy cause for a day.
- Sell your excess inventory on eBay and donate the proceeds to a charity.
- Do a food drive in your company once a month and donate the food to a food bank or a family.
- Host a blood drive at your office.

- Get involved in community projects that help the elderly or invalid.
- Give bonuses to the employees that do the most for your community.
- Donate your office resources to a charity that needs them. Let the charities use your computers, printers, and so on, until they can support themselves.
- Adopt a homeless family.
- Adopt a family relocating to your city from a war-torn country.
- Donate your old office furnishings to a charity that can give them to people who have no furnishings.
- Give your customers an opportunity to donate a dollar with every sale to a charity that you support.
- Put a donation button on your web site and have the donations go to the charity of your choice.
- Donate products or services.
- Give every employee one paid hour a week that they can use for charity.
- Use your imagination; there a million ways you can help.

The real issue isn't whether you can help or not; it is setting the time aside to do it. Your business benefits more than you can imagine from the help you give. You become more visible in the community. Your employees are more fulfilled and they talk about what a great place they work at. You become a company that is more desirable by better employees because you share strong beliefs. You make connections in the community you wouldn't otherwise and have access to things that may have otherwise eluded you.

The hour you spend on charity will pay you back in more ways than you can possibly imagine. If you are already spending an hour or more a week volunteering, or if you are already doing charity work, spend another hour in intense focus on what you can do to leverage your business and employees to create an even better opportunity to help.

Remember, you don't have to go broke doing charity; you just have to do it whether you spend a dime or not. Invest your charity hour wisely. Ask yourself these questions to determine where to start:

- What causes or ideas am I passionate about?
- If I could help anyone in the world, who would I help?
- If I could do anything to raise money to help, what would I do?
- What charitable activity can I create that is unique and important to me?
- What is a community event that helps the needy in my community in which I could get my employees involved, whether I have to pay them or if they'll donate the time?
- Do I want to help families? Individuals? Children? Animals?
- What is the one thing that has kept me from giving back? What can I do right now to overcome that obstacle?
- If I can do nothing else, can I ask everyone in the company to contribute some canned food that we can donate as a team to the local food bank?

By asking those simple questions you'll be well on your way to developing a program for giving back that will pay you back for the rest of your life. The help you give someone today is the comfort you'll have when you look back over your life. Make your business a business of meaning and a breeding ground for goodness. You'll never be sorry for any hour you invest in such a worthy endeavor.

One-Hour Action Plan

What Specifically Do I Want to Accomplish?

Give something back to my community or humanity.

What Specifically Am I Going to Do to Give Back?

- Identify a cause, charity, or activity.
- Evaluate the information collected from the previous questions and work through the answers to fully understand why I am undertaking this action and what I must do to be successful.
- List the specific steps that are necessary to achieve the desired result.
- Add deadlines to each step.
- Note who will be involved in or responsible for each step if others are to be involved.
- Allocate and schedule the time for this action plan and associated steps to be implemented.
- How will you define success so we know that you've been successful?
- What is the one action step you can take this very moment that will initiate this action plan?

Business Hour 9— The Final Hour

In the final hour of focus we are going to work on creating systems. Systemizing your business is a very powerful tool for two reasons. First, it allows you to focus quickly and easily because you don't have to create a new plan each time you work on a specific project. Second, it allows anyone who needs to go through the process in your absence to have all the information they need to complete the process.

Small businesses are particularly likely not to have systems in place to run their business. The owners often refuse to take time to create a system because the amount of time required seems to be too high compared to the actual return. Small business owners are not the only people guilty of this thinking error—so are many managers. The more and better systems you create, the better your business runs.

What Should Be Systemized

By carefully evaluating your company you should be able to find many areas (virtually all areas can be systemized) that will most quickly benefit

from systemization. Start with your own daily tasks and work your way
down. You don't have to create the systems; in many cases the systems already exist and are working. You simply need to be sure that someone is
documenting the system so that, if needed, someone else could follow the
system and replicate the results.

How to Create Effective Systems

Effective systems are created by defining the process necessary to complete
an action from creation to completion. The more specific and detailed you
can be, the more predictable the outcome. Start by documenting systems
that are working and then move to systems that need to be fine-tuned or
created. Once you've had some experience documenting existing systems,
it is much easier to create a new system. There are six steps to creating an
effective system.

1. Clearly identify the system or process.
2. Identify the outcome of performing the system or process.
3. Identify who should run the system or process.
4. Identify the exact steps involved in performing the process.
5. Identify expected outcomes at the end of each step.
6. Identify the confirmation signal that the system is complete.

Clearly Identify the System or Process

The more clearly you can identify what system or process you are documenting, the higher the likelihood of predictable success. Documenting
your manufacturing process, for example, is a good place to start, but is very
general. In addition, you'd say, "We are going to document the raw material
acquisition piece of our manufacturing process, and then move forward and

identify all other individual processes and document those in order to come up with a complete documentation of our manufacturing process."

Identify the Outcome of Performing the System or Process

Simply document what the person going through the process can expect to occur as a result of his actions. By knowing what to expect, people going through the process can be sure they have chosen the right process to follow.

Identify Who Should Run the System or Process

Your documentation should be very clear about who is authorized to use the system or run the process. It should indicate each person by name, title, or job description and specify who else needs to be involved, contacted, consulted, or informed about the process. Systems work best when everyone who needs to be involved is aware and focused at the same or appropriate time. They can also provide critical insight to people who are new to the process and running it for the first time.

Identify the Exact Steps Involved in Performing the Process

This is the most critical step of the systemization process. Be sure that you identify all steps necessary and the precise order in which they must be performed to accomplish the task. Be very methodical in your analysis of the process and the necessary steps. Be sure to include any timing or other issues that are tied to successful completion. Think of this as writing your recipe for success. If you miss a step big or small during this part of the process, future outcomes will be unpredictable.

Identify the Expected Outcomes at the End of Each Step

It is very important to document what to expect at the end of each step. By documenting milestones, anyone performing the task can have instant verification that they've done the task correctly and are getting the expected results.

Identify the Confirmation Signal that the Process Is Complete

Clearly identify how the person going through the task will know that they've completed the process and that they've achieved the appropriate outcome. Often this is where a documented system will breakdown. The person responsible for learning or initiating the system or process will go through the steps, but he won't be sure that he has achieved the desired result, so he will continue to try to apply the process after it is complete, or he will stop before he gets the desired result. Give good feedback about how these people can measure their success and how they'll know when to stop or to move to the next process.

What to Do Once You've Documented Your Systems

The purpose of documenting the system is to make running your business and the core processes of the business predictable and easy to replicate. Systemization ensures that the job is done correctly and the same way each time. Systems take away guesswork.

You should develop an overall system book that describes all the functions in your business and process-specific system books. For example, Sales would have their systems book, Marketing would have theirs, Manufacturing would have theirs. Anyone in any department who was unclear about how to do something would be able to quickly learn how to perform the process. The book should be a literal binder or other tool that is easy to access and use.

How to Use Your System Books

There are many ways to use your systems, but here are a few of the best uses of your system books.

- *To train new employees.* The system book allows new employees to learn their job and the expected performance levels of their job much more quickly. It also provides a ready resource if they need clarification on a particular issue or process.
- *To interview potential employees.* Interviewers can question potential employees about processes using the information gathered from the book.
- *To manage existing employees.* If you are having difficulty with production, processes, or predictable performance from an employee, the system books can help the employee get back on track and reinforce the standard of expected performance.
- *To improve company efficiency.* By going back to the book and evaluating the processes regularly, you can immediately pick up on necessary improvements or correct areas where people have gone off track.
- *To open new offices or divisions.* If you'll be duplicating any of the processes that you perform in your main location at another location, you already have a game plan for getting everyone up and running fast.
- *To evaluate problem areas.* If a system begins to fail, you can quickly go through the steps and assumptions that lead to the process to determine what needs to change.

- *To allow someone else to take over if necessary.* If you have a sudden change in management, sickness, or other catastrophic reason that a key player in the organization changes, you have a guidebook that someone can pick up and use to recreate success.

What Can Be Systemized?

Virtually any area of your business can be systemized; you simply have to look at the business at its component level and decide where to start. Here are some of the most obvious areas where you could start systemization. Begin by having people in those areas document how they do their job; then fine-tune the process to develop the documented system.

Marketing

Accounting

Accounts Payable

Accounts Receivable

Inventory

Manufacturing

Human Resources

Sales

Delivery

Customer Service

Spend the next hour looking at your business and deciding where to document your first system. The more time you spend in creating systems early, the less time you'll spend solving problems later. Systems equal predictability and predictability equals profit!

One-Hour Action Plan

What Specifically Do I Want to Accomplish?

Systemize my business.

What Specifically Am I Going to Do to Identify the First Area to Systemize?

- Evaluate my company and define the areas that would most benefit from systemization.
- Identify who needs to be involved in documenting the systems in each area.
- Educate my staff about the expectations for documenting systems in their organization and give them the necessary tools including a copy of this book so that they can complete the process.
- Clearly identify which systems I need to personally document.
- List the specific steps that are necessary to achieve the desired result.
- Add deadlines to each step.
- Allocate and schedule the time for this action plan and associated steps to be implemented.
- How will you define success so we know that you've been successful?
- What is the one action step you can take this very moment that will initiate this action plan?

CHAPTER 23

Call It a Day

It's that time. You've invested a few hours reading this book and, if you've followed the plan completely, you've invested at least 18 weeks of focus in transforming your life or business. I know you'd like this to be the end of the road, but it is really just the beginning. You've developed a powerful skill of focus and implementation; now it is time to continue to explore.

The focus areas that I identified for you in the previous chapters were simply a place for you to start. They gave you practical experience that allowed you to focus on larger, more obvious areas of your business and life. Now it is up to you to find the additional areas that require your newly acquired skill set.

Make your powerful hour of focus a ritual; do it without fail. Set a time, a place, an atmosphere that defines your power hour and totally immerse yourself in it each time you initiate focus.

Other Power Hours

Let's take a look at some other areas that you can focus on to create massive change. These are just a jumping-off point—I want you to add more to your list as you expand your ability to focus.

- Handling difficult employees
- Effective interpersonal communication

- Accounting systems
- Your public image
- Any skill you want to develop
- A new hobby
- Organization
- Employee development
- Improving your health or fitness level
- Researching new products to add to your mix
- Developing a new channel of distribution
- Reading
- Writing your own book

The list goes on and on, but it is up to you to pick what is most interesting and meaningful to you. The key is doing it and doing it consistently.

I look forward to sharing many more ideas with you over the coming months and years. Please go to www.powerofanhour.com and sign up for my newsletter, read the blog, and stay in touch. I want to hear from you. Tell me about your successes and experiences related to applying Fearsome Focus for an hour.

Remember this most important key as you move forward. You don't have to do everything yourself. The more you focus and leverage your hours by enlisting the help of others to accomplish your goals, the more effective you'll be in powering every hour. Manage your hours by managing your resources. The more hours you spend focused on directing the outcomes of many other hours occurring simultaneously the more you'll achieve. Pass this book on to your people, so that they can achieve more in their lives and so that they can best and most appropriately support you.

Your very next hour is waiting for you to power it up. What are you going to do next?

Index